FROM HOLY POWER
TO
HOLY PROFITS

The Black Church and
Community Economic Empowerment

FROM HOLY POWER
TO
HOLY PROFITS

The Black Church and
Community Economic Empowerment

Dr. Walter Malone, Jr.

African American Images
Chicago, Illinois

Cover illustration by Reginald Mackey

Copyright © 1994 by Walter Malone, Jr.

First Edition, First Printing

Printed in the United States of America

ISBN: 0-913543-38-1

DEDICATION

To my parents, Walter, Sr. and Marie Malone, who nurtured me with lots of Black self-determination.

ACKNOWLEDGEMENTS

I appreciate the investment and encouragement I have received from many people in the development of this project. I would like to offer my sincerest thanks to:

... the United Theological Seminary family, in particular my mentors, Drs. Samuel D. Proctor and Otis Moss, who provided me with the intellectual challenge and guidance necessary for critical thinking and research,

... the pastors and religious leaders who participated in the case studies, as well as the seminar leaders who shared in the educational forums,

... my typists, Marian Vasser and Toni Jackson, who labored day and night in typing this document,

... my Administrative Assistant, Eugene McCormick, whose support and commitment gave me the freedom to give my total being to this project,

... the congregation of the Canaan Missionary Baptist Church for their prayers and support of my ministry,

... the publisher and production staff at African American Images for their encouragement and support,

and finally,

... my parents, Walter, Sr. and Marie Malone; my sisters, Deborah and Wanda, for their encouragement; and my wife, Sandra, and son, Walter III, for their love, sacrifices, and encouragement.

FOREWORD

In the year 2020, Dr. Walter Malone, Jr. will be an energetic 65 years old. He will have played a pivotal role in helping to determine the direction of the African American church and community in the twenty-first century. The African American church and community economic empowerment are two of our great streams of Black liberation. The model of Canaan Missionary Baptist Church, under the leadership of Dr. Malone, will be a spiritual flagship and national resource center. It will have established the vision, ministry and focus for economic development as one of the necessary liberation themes and paths.

It has been one of the great joys of my ministry to serve as co-mentor, with Dr. Samuel Dewitt Proctor, for Rev. Malone's Doctor of Ministry class of 1993 at United Theological Seminary in Dayton, Ohio. In addition to serving as co-mentor, I observed Dr. Malone's ministry in Louisville, Kentucky, where he is now in his eleventh year as pastor of this young and growing congregation. His congregation is responding to his leadership in this audacious and redeeming experiment of reviving and enhancing a community through the development of a new congregation that confronts economic injustice.

In the next 25 years, this young and dynamic congregation will have a significant number of parents and grandparents who will have participated in this bold contextual theological enterprise, and their shoulders will be the foundations and bridges for a new generation. While the congregation will still be less than forty years old, their Africentric, Christocentric theology and lifestyle will be a global witness for majoring in the impossible.

The African American church has always been a house of liberation, education, culture, family, integrity and spirituality. Morehouse College was born in the basement of the Springfield

Baptist Church of Augusta, Georgia. Spelman College was born in the Friendship Baptist Church of Atlanta, Georgia. Atlanta Life Insurance Company was born in Wheat Street Baptist Church of Atlanta, Georgia. And the movement led by Dr. Martin Luther King, Jr. was born in the Black churches of Montgomery, Alabama, and the deep South. Dr. Malone follows a great liberation tradition as he leads Canaan to the promised land along paths of theological liberation witnessed by economic development and community empowerment. Christ is at the center of this excellent, dynamic spiritual action.

Generations present and future will join me in welcoming this document - this writing - about a dream no longer deferred, and a vision that must be shared within and beyond the boundaries of the African American community. Christ Jesus lives in the ministry, vision and mission of Canaan Missionary Baptist Church, and Dr. Walter Malone is a living testimony.

Dr. Otis Moss, Jr., Pastor
Olivet Institutional Baptist Church
Cleveland, Ohio

CONTENTS

INTRODUCTION

The problem of economic injustice is an issue confronting people around the world, particularly African Americans. In his book *Two Nations: Black and White, Separate, Hostile, Unequal,* Andrew Hacker speaks definitively about this crisis in the African American community.

We are reminded that the name The United States of America is an idea, not a reality. The reality of America is that it is composed of two nations, one White and one Black. From the time African people were imported to this country as slaves, they have been excluded from the mainstream of society. African Americans today are still treated as aliens in this country. White America's pervasive and penetrating economic, educational, political, and social systems were designed to keep Black America in a position of subordination. Hacker, a White professor of political science at Queens College, states that

Black men, women, and children were brought to this country for a singular purpose: to work. Indeed, the demand for their labor was so great that slaves continued to be smuggled in even after that traffic had been banned by the Constitution. In the years following emancipation, former slaves found that their services would not necessarily be needed. Their labor, like that of other Americans, would be subject to the vagaries of a market economy. The capitalist system has been frank in admitting that it cannot always create jobs for everyone who wants to work. This economic reality has certainly been a pervasive fact of Black life. For as long as records have been kept, in good times and bad, White America has ensured that the unemployment imposed on Blacks will be approximately double those experienced by Whites. Stated very simply, if you are Black in America, you will find it twice as hard to find or keep a job.[1]

1

The Black Liberation Church views its ministry of economic justice as part of its overall mission to liberate people from anyone, or anything, that oppresses them in this world. The Bible declares that God desires people to experience wholeness in life. Jesus said, "The thief cometh not, but for to steal, and to kill, and to destroy: I am come that they might have life, and that they might have it more abundantly." Since God desires people to experience wholeness in life, the Black Liberation Church seeks to minister to people in a wholistic manner. The Black Liberation Church recognizes the authenticity of ministering to people physically, spiritually, mentally, emotionally, and economically.

There seems to be a paradox concerning the economic status of America. On one hand, the country is seen as one of the economic giants of the world. But, on the other hand, America appears to be standing on shaky economic ground. When compared to many other countries around the world, the United States is certainly an economic giant. The American economy has grown to provide a luxurious standard of living for many of its citizens. Most people around the world have never experienced a three bedroom house, a car, and three meals a day. In industry, agriculture, technology, and trade, America is certainly among the top power nations of the world. Through its governmental system, there is some support provided for education, access to food, unemployment compensation, and social security during our golden years.

However, when one looks at the American economy from another perspective and views the growing number of people in this country who are poor, unemployed, homeless, hungry, and sick standing hopelessly on the steps of churches, service agencies, and shelters, one gets the picture of an economic system that is marked by injustice. In a pastoral letter written by the National Conference of Catholic Bishops on the subject

2

of economic justice we are told that

> harsh poverty plagues our country despite its great wealth. More than 33 million Americans are poor; by any reasonable standard, another 20 to 30 million are needy. Poverty is increasing in the United States, not decreasing. For a people who believe in progress, this should be cause for alarm. These burdens fall most heavily on Blacks, Hispanics, and Native Americans. Even more disturbing is the large increase in the number of women and children living in poverty. Today children are the largest single group among the poor. This tragic fact seriously threatens the nation's future. That so many people are poor in a nation as rich as ours is a social and moral scandal that we cannot ignore.[2]

Not since the 1930's during the "Great Depression" has our nation's economy been on such shaky ground. For the past several decades, we have not been able to control inflation nor the deficits in the national budget. For the first time in her history, the United States has become the world's major debtor nation. The signs are all present that our country is grappling with a weak and vacillating economy. Farmers are in despair as they try to make a living and keep their land. Major steel mills have closed. The closings of corporations like Eastern Airlines and other financial institutions as well as the savings and loan scandal have raised the consciousness of Americans; we are beginning to understand the problematic status of our economy.

Paul L. Wachtel addresses this economic dilemma from another angle in *The Poverty of Affluence*. The economic dilemma of America was not caused by a shortage of resources; rather, our problems stem from the mentality we exercise in relationship to available resources. Every generation feels that it ought to have more than the previous generation. Materialism and consumerism have become such a part of the American way of life that we can never get enough. Wachtel clarifies this idea of "the poverty of affluence" when he states:

> Our present problems stem not so much from physical and economic limits - real as those are - as from our miscalculations as to what really works to provide us with security and satisfaction. Our economic system and our relation with nature has gone haywire because we have lost track of what we really need. Increasing numbers of middle-class Americans are feeling pressured and deprived not because of their economic situation per se - we remain an extraordinarily affluent society - but because we have placed an impossible burden on the economic dimension of our lives. So long as we persist in defining our well-being predominantly in economic terms and in relying on our economic considerations to provide us with our primary frame of reference for personal and social policy decisions, we will remain unsatisfied.[3]

America's economic system is characterized by instability and tainted by injustice. The philosophy and practice of capitalism dictate that some people will always be excluded from the financial resources of our society. This has been the painful plight of Black people in America. White America got rich during the dark days of slavery, yet Black people were never given their fair share of opportunities for economic growth in this country. How disturbing it is that in the 1991 "State Of Black America" address, published by the National Urban League, the economic status of African Americans would be spoken of as "permanent poverty and inequality."

In stating this case David H. Swinton declares,

This latest review of the economic status of African Americans reveals that the pattern of persisting economic disadvantage continues. The long recovery in progress since the recession of 1982 has had little impact on the intensity of racial inequality in economic life. Indeed, by many measures, even though we are at the peak of the longest recovery in the last five decades, the degree of racial inequality is higher as we begin the 1990's than at any other time in the last 20 years. Moreover, recent evidence suggests that we are about to enter another period of economic slowdown. If this downturn has an impact similar to the last few recessions, African Americans will bear a disproportionate share of its hardships. Moreover, they will not regain all of the lost ground in the subsequent recovery. Thus, the long-run impact will be further erosion in the already disadvantaged economic status of Blacks.[4]

The disadvantaged economic status of African Americans appears to be a permanent feature of the American economy because the economic system of this country was designed to keep African Americans, for the most part, out of economic power. Studies reveal that White America, both individually and collectively as family units, receives more income than Black America.

The fact that Blacks receive only three-fifths as much income per person as Whites creates enormous income gaps. In 1989, Blacks had an income deficit equal to $6,149 for every man, woman, and child. In the aggregate, the income of the African American population was $186 billion short of the income required for parity.[5]

The Canaan Missionary Baptist Church is located in the Algonquin Parkway community in Louisville, Kentucky. As pastor of the Canaan Church, I believe that economic justice is essential to the wholistic ministry of the Canaan Church. The economic plight of African Americans in Louisville, Kentucky is marked by the same kind of economic deprivation that African Americans are experiencing across the country. In the city of Louisville, the majority of White people live in the East end, while the majority of African Americans live in the West end. The East end is characterized by economic development, while the West end suffers economic deprivation. In the East end, there are several restaurants, theaters, shopping centers, and a host of other businesses. There are stable houses, and new homes are being built on a regular basis. In the West end, there are no major restaurants, theaters, or shopping centers. There are very few businesses, and abandoned houses stand on several streets. There are few opportunities for employment and entrepreneurship. The unemployment rate of African Americans in Louisville is twice the rate of White people.

In Algonquin Parkway, the average annual income per home is approximately $20,000. The Algonquin Parkway Community Needs Assessment Study indicated that,

> By 1980, about 6,845 more Blacks lived in the area while the White population declined by 13,027 persons, to only about 3,249 persons. Accordingly, the portion of Black population increased from 36.9% to 83.4% of the total study area population between 1960 and 1980. The median income for all families in the study area fell sharply from 102.4% of the city median in 1950 to only 72.3% of the city median in 1980. About 40% of the total population in the study area lives below the poverty level.[6]

The economic deprivation with which the African American community struggles because of economic and social injustice continues to limit the resources necessary for family livelihood, depriving the community of its rightful place in the mainstream of America's market economy. "Many of the so-

6

cial pathologies, such as family deterioration, high crime rates, low educational attainment, and excessive death rates are undoubtedly related to the huge income deficits."[7]

A faith statement, or mission statement, helps a local congregation to keep before them their reason for existing. It also speaks of their particular calling in light of their social setting. The mission statement of the Canaan Church says that the "Canaan Missionary Baptist Church is a loving and caring congregation that seeks to build and strengthen the lives of people through the liberating ministry of Jesus Christ." Our emphasis on building the lives of people is an effort to be faithful to the servant theology mandated by Christ; for he said, "The Son of man came not to be ministered unto, but to minister and to give His life as a ransom for many" (Mark 10:45). As such, Christian education, evangelism, liberation, economic empowerment, and social justice form the cornerstone of our mission.

This mission statement describes, in a concise manner, both what the Canaan Church seeks to be and seeks not to be. Every church has its own unique personality and character, which is determined by its theological understanding, or its belief system. People act out what they think, and they think about their beliefs.

Within our contemporary society there are two types of Black churches. The first one I call the "sanctuary-bound, non-liberation church." This church fails to see that God is involved in all of life, thus worship is relegated only to the sanctuary. It has bought deeply into the Western theological idea that life is divided into sacred and secular dimensions. It fails to recognize that in Hebrew and African thought, all of life is sacred.

The non-liberation Black church is only concerned about going to heaven. There is no theological understanding of the kingdom of God being realized in the right now. In the words of Elton Trueblood, they see the church as having only marginal relevancy, and not major relevancy.

The second type of Black church that exists in our society is the "liberation church." This church defines salvation as deliverance from personal sin and corporate sin. It takes the theological position that in our salvation experience, God desires our liberation from anyone, or anything, that seeks to oppress us in this world. The liberation church believes in evangelization and emancipation. Thus worship is viewed not only as an encounter with God in the sanctuary, but also as a call and challenge to get involved in community life.

The liberation church uses the expression "wholistic ministry" because it seeks to minister to people spiritually, physically, mentally, emotionally, socially, and economically. The liberation church understands that there cannot be a sense of spiritual wholeness in the community without addressing the issues of social justice and economic empowerment. It is this type of Black church that will be illustrated throughout this book.

Chapter 1 presents a theological perspective on economic justice. I will lift up from both Old and New Testament stories, institutions and themes that declare God's intention for economic justice. Here I seek to show how the idea of redemption includes economic justice and the church's purpose of establishing community.

Chapter 2 gives a historical account of the Black liberation church's involvement in economic justice. We will see how the Black liberation church originated cooperative economics within the African American community.

Chapter 3 explains the idea of revolution from a Christian perspective and shows its relationship to the Black liberation church's ministry. I will discuss visions of economic empowerment by three Black religious leaders and the value of a coalition of approaches. This chapter concludes with an explanation of the meaning and importance of *The Pedagogy of the*

Oppressed in implementing visions for economic empowerment.

Chapter 4 presents case studies of nine African American religious institutions that presently have ministries of economic empowerment. The purpose of this chapter is to show the validity and the practicality of this kind of ministry in the life of the Black liberation church as we move toward the twenty-first century. I will also discuss how these models helped to shape the development of my church's economic ministry. These studies should be of value to churches that seek to develop their own economic ministries.

Chapter 5 offers a description of my church's program, which is called Canaan's Community Development Corporation. I will discuss its purpose, philosophy, and development as well as some of our projects, including an eight-week session on economic justice, Church Family Expos, and the Computer Training Program.

This study of the ministry of economic empowerment is critical as we prepare to minister to the Black Church in the twenty-first century.

CHAPTER I

A Theological Perspective of Economic Justice

The Biblical record speaks of God's activity and involvement in history in bringing the world and mankind back into a state of blessed wholeness. This idea of blessed wholeness concerns humanity being in right relationship with God as Creator, and with each other. Humanity is to worship and love God; likewise, we have the responsibility to love, respect and care for one another. When asked by a certain lawyer one day, "Which is the great commandment in the law?" Jesus responded by saying,

> Thou shalt love the Lord thy God with all thy heart, and with all thy soul, and with all thy mind. This is the first and greatest commandment. And the second is like unto it, Thou shalt love thy neighbor as thyself. On these two commandments hang all the law and the prophets. Matthew 22:35-40

The Genesis account of creation speaks of a world, including humanity, that is characterized by togetherness and wholeness. Because humanity was made in the image of God, man and woman stand as the summit of God's creation. It was to humanity that God entrusted the stewardship of God's created order. "And God blessed them, and God said unto them, Be fruitful, and multiply, and replenish the earth, and subdue it: and have dominion over the fish of the sea, and over the fowl of the air, and over every living thing that moveth upon the earth" (Genesis 1:28). The Genesis record also speaks of Adam and Eve disrupting God's design by trying to deny their status as creatures. With the entrance of sin into the world, humanity is alienated from God and from one another.

> Sin simultaneously alienates human beings from God and shatters the solidarity of the human community. Yet this reign of sin is not the final word. The primeval history is followed by the call of Abraham, a man of faith, who was to be the bearer of the promise to many nations (Genesis 12:1-4). Throughout the Bible, we find this struggle between sin and repentance.[8]

Salvation is God's initiative to bring wholeness back into the created order. It is meant to save humanity from its inhumanity. God desires to save us from anything that oppresses us—including economic injustice—and that works against the solidarity of the human community.

At various times in the Biblical record when God's nature and will for humanity is revealed, there is a divine intervention to liberate the poor and oppressed. The story of the Exodus is one such example. When Moses, a representative of Yahweh, is called in the Midian Desert to go back to Egypt to tell Pharaoh to "Let my people go," God's position is manifested against oppression and injustice. God said to Moses,

> I have seen the affliction of my people who are in Egypt, and have heard their cry because of their taskmasters; I know their sufferings, and I have come down to deliver them out of the hand of the Egyptians. Exodus 3:7-8

The deliverance of the children of Israel was part of, or was relative to, the covenant God made with Abraham, Isaac, and Jacob.

12

However, the Exodus served more than one purpose. We must be careful not to separate the spiritual emphasis of this story from its social implications. In the Exodus, God also acted to end economic oppression and slavery as well as build community. The covenant at Mt. Sinai and the giving of the Ten Commandments were in part a follow-up to God's desire for solidarity and economic justice. At Mt. Sinai, the children of Israel were reminded that it was Yahweh who had freed them from slavery and economic oppression; they were to relate to one another and others now as a kingdom of priests. There is an emphasis here on the importance of and care for community. The idea of community implies that there is to be wholeness and solidarity. The Ten Commandments were given to provide the children of Israel with the discipline necessary to act justly toward each other as a new community in the land of Canaan. Ronald J. Sider speaks of the significance of the Ten Commandments in identifying God as one who is concerned about the liberation of the oppressed.

> The preamble to the Ten Commandments, probably the most important portion of the entire law for Israel, begins with this same revolutionary truth. Before he gives the two tables of the law, Yahweh identifies himself: "I am the Lord your God, who brought you out of the land of Egypt, out of the house of bondage." (Deuteronomy 5:6; Exodus 20:2) Yahweh is the one who frees from bondage. The God of the Bible wants to be known as the liberator of the oppressed.[9]

Although the children of Israel strove to build a new community of faith after their deliverance, they became susceptible to the idolatry of greed; they began to perpetuate economic injustice against each other. As God was against Pharaoh in Egypt, God was also against the house of Israel for their social injustice and economic oppression. During the middle of the eighth century B.C., political success and economic prosperity in Israel reached a zenith. It was at this moment in history that God sent prophets like Isaiah, Jeremiah, Amos, and Micah to speak against Israel because it had become wealthy by oppressing the poor. Both Isaiah and Amos reminded Israel that God demanded more than formalism and ritualism in worship. God demands justice for the poor and oppressed, and without this, Israel's worship was not acceptable (Isaiah 1:13,17; Amos 5:21-24).

The prophet Micah addresses the problem of economic injustice in a concise manner by declaring, "He hath shown thee, O man, what is good; and what doth the Lord require of thee, but to do justly, and to love mercy, and to walk humbly with thy God?" (Micah 6:8) The prophet Micah speaks out against the Jerusalem government for abusing and exploiting the poor. He calls for a change in the social system, particularly a redistribution of goods. "To do justly" in this text is speaking of economic justice. "To love mercy" speaks of God's desire for abiding solidarity. "To walk humbly with thy God" means having the faith that allows solidarity or community to exist. Walter Brueggemann speaks of this text from Micah "as voices of the night —against justice" by saying,

> First, the poetry addresses social power. They are the ones who have arranged things the way they are. They are also the ones who benefit from the way things are. Second, the agenda is consistently economic. The real issues concerning justice have to do with access to and control of life-goods. We have so much to learn yet about this as the proper agenda of the Bible, and, indeed, as the proper agenda of God. That agenda has been on God's mind since the Exodus. Third, address to leadership and concern for economics make clear that Micah is making a critique of the system of social control. This is not poetry that simply strikes out at a specific act. It is a much

more sustained analysis based on the legal precedent of the Torah to show that the entire social system is wrongly directed. So the invitation to do justice is in a context of the systemic power of evil.[10]

The Jubilee Principle in the Old Testament is a direct example of God's desire for economic equity among all people. Every fifty years all slaves were to be set free, and all land returned to its original owners without cost. Land was a primary means of gaining wealth in Israel. When the children of Israel first entered the promised land, all the land had been divided on an equal basis among the tribes. But because of death, physical handicaps, and other social dilemmas, some people would become poorer than others. God instituted the Jubilee Principle to ensure an equitable distribution of land ownership every fifty years. The Jubilee Principle did not abolish private property, but it did provide equity as a means of acquiring wealth (Leviticus 25:10-24).

During the Old Testament period, the poor were the landless, the social outcasts, and the dispossessed. The codes in Exodus, Leviticus, and Deuteronomy speak of the poor as it concerns their social and economic plight. The wealthy, in contrast, were landowners who had elite membership status in the community.

In an article entitled "The Biblical Tradition of the Poor and Martin Luther King, Jr.," Thomas Hoyt, Jr. states,

Deuteronomy 15:4 proclaims, 'There ought to be no poor man in your midst.' Of course, this admonition implies that there were poor people. We have pointed out that the Israelites in their semi-nomadic state probably favored the nomadic ideal which recognized no gulf between the rich and poor. With settlement in Canaan, sociological shock took place. There were still those in the agricultural life of Canaan who came to the rescue of their brothers in distress, but there were many individuals who turned to the competitive spirit, which in turn led to exploitation of their countrymen. The Deuteronomic writer was probably influenced by this semi-nomadic ideal and the remembrance of the covenant. Yahweh had promised that Israel would prosper and this prosperity would extend to each and every Israelite if the covenant would be kept inviolate. In other words, one of the main features of the covenant was the total elimination of poverty. Thus, the very existence of poor people in Israel would be considered a sign of covenant violation.[11]

There was a consistent admonition in the codes for the poor to receive special consideration, indicating that they had a right to the fruits of the land (Deut. 10:18; 15:11; 24:17; Ex. 22:19-26; Lev. 19:9-10; Deut. 24:19-21). In Canaan, Israel had the responsibility of establishing community. It was to be an inclusive community where the widows, orphans, and sojourners would all be cared for.

In the New Testament, God's desire for wholeness and solidarity among people is vividly manifested in the person of Jesus Christ. In His ministry, Jesus stood against all forms of social injustice and oppression.

> In Jesus Christ, God takes the form of "the other" as a member of an oppressed race, an exploited class, and a colonized nation. God, in Jesus Christ, becomes poor and oppressed. The paradox and scandal of the incarnation is that God takes the form of a servant and makes himself one with 'the others.'[12]

Jesus was born not in a palace but in a manger. His parents were so poor they could not bring the normal offering for purification, which was a lamb; so instead they brought two pigeons to the temple. Jesus had no regular income during his public ministry. On one occasion when some people were eager to follow him, Jesus warned them, "Foxes have holes, and birds of the air have nests; but the Son of man has no where to lay his head" (Matthew 8:20). In his preaching and teaching,

16

Jesus revealed his sensitivity to the poor and his stand against economic injustice.

In the inaugurational message that Jesus delivered at the beginning of his ministry, he emphatically stated that he had an agenda for the oppressed. And on this agenda was economics — "He hath anointed me to preach the gospel to the poor" (Luke 4:18-19). Jesus Christ was a social activist whose ministry of liberation was designed to minister to the total person. This message in the gospel of Luke not only describes the ministry of Christ, it also describes the ministry of the church that claims to give allegiance to Jesus Christ.

The early church we read about in the Book of Acts gave expression to the kind of wholeness and solidarity God desires among humanity. Their understanding of the need for economic justice is evidenced by the fact that they were characterized as "having all things common, and selling their possessions so that no one in the community would be in need" (Acts 2:44-45). The Catholic Bishop's letter on economic justice states that

> the early community at Jerusalem distributed its possessions so that "there was no needy person among them," and held "all things in common" - a phrase that suggests not only shared material possessions, but more fundamentally, friendship and mutual concern among all its members. (Acts 4:32-34; 2:44) While recognizing the dangers of wealth, the early church proposed the proper use of possessions to alleviate need and suffering, rather than universal dispossession.[13]

In the letters of the Apostle Paul, reference is made to our responsibility toward the poor. Particularly in 1st Corinthians, theological significance is given to the fact that many of the church members come from lower social orders. God has chosen the poor, the powerless, and the humble to serve in the kingdom. By choosing the poor and powerless in this manner, values are reversed. Those of high estate are brought low, and those of low estate are brought high. All human marks of distinction are superseded. (1st Corinthians 1:26-29)

It is in this same letter that Paul criticizes the church at Corinth for its treatment of the poor. In chapter eleven, Paul speaks of how certain members of the church were creating a spirit of division around the Lord's Supper. At a celebration known as the "Love Feast," the rich were not sharing their food and drink with the poor. By neglecting the needs of the poor, Paul accuses the rich of being class-conscious rather than Christ-conscious. (1st Corinthians 11:22)

The Apostle Paul refers to "the poor saints which are at Jerusalem" in his letter to the church at Rome and Galatia (Rom. 15:26; Gal. 2:10). Scholars are not sure whether Paul uses this term as an honorary title, or whether the community was in fact materially poor. Aquinata Bockmann argues that

> the poor and the slaves outside the Christian community are not taken into consideration in Paul's letters. He does not really develop the idea that Christians should endeavor to create a more just social order. This is presumably due to the fact that Christians form a minority recruited mostly from the lower social orders, and to the fact that the end of the world is expected at any moment.[14]

Although Paul's letters indicated that he was expecting the immediate return of Jesus Christ, his counsel to the various churches evidences concern for social and economic justice. To the church at Philippi he said, "Let this mind be in you, which was also in Christ Jesus" (Philippians 2:5). As an interpreter of the mind of Christ, Paul understood that the Christian faith was to be expressed both vertically and horizontally. He was fully aware of Jesus' concern for the poor and the oppressed. Throughout his letters, Paul speaks of the importance of having both commitment to God and care for one another.

Redemptive history is a continuous manifestation of God's plan for a new community. Because of sin, God's idea of community was, and still is, disrupted. Brokenness and alienation are descriptive of the painful plight of humanity. The disorder and fragmentation of our world can be illustrated in the familiar lines of the nursery rhyme:

> Humpty Dumpty sat on a wall.
> Humpty Dumpty had a great fall.
> All the king's horses and all the King's men
> couldn't put Humpty Dumpty back together again.

In Jesus Christ, God desires to bring all of humanity together to constitute a new community. A community that is in fellowship with God provides for all of our needs. There are enough resources available for all of humanity. Economic justice has to do with everyone having his/her rightful share of God's resources in the world community. In his book, *Stewards Shaped By Grace: The Church's Gift to a Troubled World*, Rhodes Thompson says,

> God's blessing provides for the needs of all the family. Ephesians uses the Greek word *oikonomia* to describe God's plan for the fullness of time (1:10) as a way of meeting the needs of all the human family. Compounded of *oikos* (house) and *nomos* (law, rule), this word signifies household management that seeks the welfare of each family member. It echoes Gandhi's belief that 'the earth has enough for everybody's need, but not enough for everybody's greed.' Of special interest to us, *oikonomia* is often translated "stewardship," as in Ephesians 3:2.[15]

God assigned Jesus the stewardship of establishing a new community. Likewise, the church must minister to a hurting humanity the message of God's desire for community as

19

revealed in the life, death, and resurrection of Jesus Christ. The primary purpose of the church is to glorify God and edify humanity. Paul speaks of the stewardship aspect of the church (as it relates to community) again in Ephesians 3:9: "And to make all men see what is the fellowship of the mystery, which from the beginning of the world hath been hid in God, who created all things by Jesus Christ." The word church in Greek, *ekklesia*, literally means "the called out ones." The church constitutes the people of God called to go out into the world and reveal God's plan of community in Christ.

No serious theology can omit the relationship of the church to our society's economy. The church's stewardship is clarified by the term *oikos*, which connotes an access to livelihood. It speaks of the way people live in the world in relation to each other, the economy, and God. M. Douglas Meeks states in his book, *God The Economist*, that

> recent research has shown the pivotal theological, liturgical, and social implications of the concept of *oikos* for the primitive Christian communities. The *oikos* or household constituted for the Christian movement as well as for its environment a chief basis, paradigm and reference point for religious and moral as well as social, political, and economic organization, interaction, and ideology. It is evident that the household had a dominant influence not only on the structure and internal conduct of the early Christian groups, but also upon their theological perspectives and socioreligious symbols.[16]

Again, it is noteworthy that we are told in the book of Acts that in the early church they "had all things common; and sold their possessions and goods, and parted them to all men, as every man had need" (Acts 2:44-45). The early church was operating under God's economy for the household. God's economy for the household is marked by inclusiveness. It includes the poor, the disinherited, and the oppressed. The early Christian community's philosophy of economics was shaped by its understanding of God's concern for justice and solidarity. The emphasis of the early church both within and outside the community was that everyone was to have his/her equal share in God's household. During the early periods of church history, this emphasis of God's economy was maintained to some degree. The vows of poverty, chastity, and obedience of religious orders during the Middle Ages did not comprise a theology that advocated any evil inherent in material goods. Rather, voluntary poverty was a discipline designed to bring one into a more focused spiritual disposition for performing the work of God.

The period of the Reformation extended this discipline to ordinary Christians to practice during their everyday lives. During the seventeenth and eighteenth centuries, the church's stewardship and theology of God's desire for economic solidarity were removed from the economic philosophy of public life. With the development of capitalism there was a change in emphasis from livelihood to exchange. Livelihood is concerned with everyone having accessibility to the resources in God's household. Exchange is concerned only with personal profit.

The contemporary church has become so accommodative to capitalism that its theology is often viewed as a justification of economic injustice. In order for the church's theology to seriously confront the economic philosophy of our society,

> theology would need, first, to unmask the claim that God is absent in the market economy by showing the presence of dominative God concepts in the ideology of the market society, and second, to point to the presence of the living God of Israel and of Jesus Christ in the struggle of those who suffer economic, political, and cultural domination.[17]

From a theological perspective, the contemporary church

21

(which includes the liberation and non-liberation church) needs to raise some serious questions concerning the economic philosophies present in our world today. Is the capitalist or socialist form of economic philosophy antagonistic to God's desire for solidarity? Does the economic system of our country lead us to idolatry? Is oppression and dehumanization an outcome of the present economic system of our country? Is God a Marxist, Socialist, Communalist, or Capitalist?

Theologically there seems to be some connectedness between the Christian faith and the Marxist view of economics. In the person of Jesus Christ, we receive the highest revelation of God's intention for human beings. Jesus is fully God, but he was also fully man. Jesus shows us how to be a real person in relationship with other people. The life and ministry of Jesus Christ was centered around lifting and liberating humanity from any form of oppression in the world.

> The driving motive of Marx's life was that men and women might recover the humanity which had been ripped from them in the very act of creating and producing their own handiwork. Marx was filled with outrage that things had come to replace persons in value. He saw humans as investing their whole reality and purpose in what is a mere fragment of themselves: the commodity.[18]

Since this book is about using liberation theology to eradicate the injustices that have been placed on African Americans, I do not want to do injustice to our history by not mentioning the concept of sharing the wealth that far predates Marxism. According to Julius Nyerere, communalism is an attitude of mind that has nothing to do with the possession or non-possession of wealth. The true African socialist never looks on one class of men as his brethren and another as his natural enemy. Nyerere goes on to explain that the needs of the community are valued over the needs of the individual. Dr. Jawanza Kunjufu explains this thought in his book, *Black Economics: Solutions for Economic and Community Empowerment.*

In rejecting the capitalist attitude of mind which colonialism brought into Africa, we must reject also the capitalist methods which go with it. One of these is the individual ownership of land. In Africa, land was always recognized as belonging to the community. Each individual within the society had a right to use the land because otherwise they could not earn a living. One cannot have the right to life without also having the right to some means of maintaining life. The Africans' right to land was simply the right to use it; he had no other right to it. Nor did it occur to him to try and claim one. The foreigner introduced a completely different concept- the concept of land as a marketable commodity. According to this system, a person could claim a piece of land as his own private property, whether he intended to use it or not. All that had to be done to gain a living from the land was to charge rent to the people who wanted to use it.

This is a fundamental change in how land was viewed in the African economy; land belonged to the extended family. In the capitalist European American economy, land belonged to the individual. This was the first downfall in the African economy. The second downfall was the introduction of money. A means of currency was used in the exchange of goods and services. Exploring our own African history, we understand that services and products were distributed among the people based on a barter system. The Kunjufu family produced yams and the Ofari family produced tomatoes. We exchanged products between each other and this was done without the use of currency.[19]

John Francis Kavanaugh uses the term "the dialectical totality" to speak of how different parts come together to make the whole. No one part can ever be fully realized as long as it is separated from the totality. Such was the case with Nyerere's communalism. Marx's position as it related to the "dialectical totality" was that all parts of our human world influence one another. The religious, political, philosophical, educational, and economic are all related to each other. But the economic (and capitalism in particular) was separated from the whole and used to dominate the lives of people. In the capitalistic system in which we live, there is an obsession for "thingification." Consumerism and materialism are the driving forces in our lives, even at the expense of dehumanizing other persons.

In the system of capitalism, there is a group that must be poor in order for there to be another group that will always be rich. This theological critique is not an attempt to destroy the system of capitalism; Marx's socialist system has not worked effectively toward economic justice either. But theologically, we must look at the capitalistic system of America and realize that, in its present form, it is not working on the basis of God's desire for community, solidarity, and economic justice. In the life and ministry of Jesus Christ, the emphasis is placed on personhood and community. In the present economic system of our country, capitalism places the emphasis on commodities. Kavanaugh illuminates this idea when he says,

> In our culture, if we aspire to live in the Personal Form, espe-
> cially as revealed in Christianity, we have to realize how the
> cultural gospel is not only an alternative to the Gospel of Jesus,
> but also a metaphysics of humanity, a philosophical worldview.
> As a worldview, as a theory of human realization, the cul-
> tural gospel perverts the fundamental exigencies of human
> identity into a denial of humanness and a denial of God. It
> offers a practically lived atheism and anti-humanism, insofar
> as it is an embodiment of the most fundamental of human
> sins: idolatry.[20]

The theology of Calvinism had a great influence in the development of capitalism. The idea of predestination in the

24

Calvinistic doctrine provided a basis for the justification of individualism. In the economic philosophy of capitalism, our society operates on the idea of "you get yours, and I'll get mine." Capitalism says only the strong survive, and the weak deserve whatever position they are in. The idea of predestination in Calvinism is that God has chosen some people to go to heaven, and God has chosen some other people to go to hell. In a wider sense, those who are rich are so because of God's predestination; likewise with the poor. Max Weber, in his book *The Protestant Ethic and the Spirit of Capitalism*, clarifies this theological posture:

> A specifically bourgeois economic ethic had grown up. With the consciousness of standing in the fullness of God's grace and being visibly blessed by [God], the bourgeois business man, as long as he remained within the bounds of formal correctness, as long as his moral conduct was spotless and the use to which he put his wealth was not objectionable, could follow his pecuniary interests as he would and feel that he was fulfilling a duty in doing so. The power of religious asceticism provided him, in addition, with sober, conscientious, and unusually industrious workmen, who clung to their work as to a life purpose willed by God.[21]

The theological position that some people are rich while others are poor simply because of God's will suggests a kind of exclusivism. Some people are rich and special with God, while others are destined to be poor and rejected. With this theological and sociological attitude, one can feel no responsibility toward the plight of the poor. Again, Weber states that,

> Calvinism opposed organic social organization in the fiscal-monopolistic form which it assumed in Anglicanism under the Stuarts, especially in the conceptions of Laud, this alliance of Church and State with the monopolists on the basis of a Christian-social ethical foundation. Its leaders were univer-

sally among the most passionate opponents of this type of politically privileged commercial, putting-out, and colonial capitalism.[22]

The Calvinistic theology that helped to develop the economic philosophy of capitalism in America stands in opposition to the ethical teachings and ministry of Jesus Christ. The ministry of Christ was centered around the theme of liberation as stated in Luke 4:18-19. Christian theology is a theology of liberation.

The idea of liberation theology is a most vital issue for the Black church and community. Conventional American theology has not seriously addressed the struggles of Black people in this country. James Cone is right when he suggests that God is not neutral; God is on the side of the oppressed. Black theology is Black people's perspective of God in light of how God is manifested in the midst of their oppressed condition. Being grounded in the liberation theology of Jesus Christ, Black theology seeks to provide the Black community with the strategy, spirit, and strength to work for its God-given freedom and rightful position in the world. In many cases, the theological and sociological perspectives and decisions made in America have been an effort to subjugate, if not destroy, Black America. Black theology demands that America move toward economic justice and solidarity.

> ...the role of Black theology is to tell Black people to focus on their own self-determination as a community by preparing to do anything which the community believes to be necessary for its existence.[23]

Howard Thurman speaks of the importance of liberation theology for Black people when he speaks of Jesus and the disinherited. Thurman tells of an experience he had in India when he was asked by a Hindu, How can you worship the same

God of the people who have oppressed your people for over three hundred years? Thurman's reply was that he could worship Jesus Christ because he and Jesus had so much in common. He spoke of Jesus' poverty at birth, his being a part of a despised people (the Jews), and the time Jesus spent with the downtrodden. The atmosphere in which Jesus was born and lived was one of oppression caused by the rule of Rome. It was not a social situation Jesus could ignore and still give meaning to life. There was a demand upon Jesus to respond to the political, social, and economic issues of his day. In *Jesus And The Disinherited*, Thurman declares,

> This is the position of the disinherited in every age. What must be the attitude toward the rulers, the controllers of political, social, and economic life? This is the question of the Negro in American life. Until he has faced and settled that question, he cannot inform his environment with reference to his own life, whatever may be his preparation or his pretensions.[24]

Theodore Walker, Jr. in his book, *Empower The People: Social Ethics for the African-American Church*, speaks of what he calls the ethic of breaking bread. In the African American church, to speak of having a right relationship with God is to speak of doing God's will. The Scripture reveals that it is through God's will that we provide adequate food, shelter, clothing, health care, freedom and other resources and opportunities for all people. (Take note of Matthew 25) To get right with God, according to Walker, is to contribute to the empowerment of the people.

This social ethic is profoundly expressed when we share together the sacrament of holy communion. The bread at communion symbolizes the basic necessities of life.

> To break bread means to share food and money and land and power and other resources, including spiritual and religious resources, with the people. The symbol of breaking bread,

27

then, provides us with a model, and a counter-model, for social behavior: the ethic of breaking bread, and the ethic of
crumbs.[25]

The story of the rich man and Lazarus in Luke 16:19-31 is
seen as an example of one who practiced the ethic of crumbs.
The rich man went to hell because he refused to share his bread
with the poor man Lazarus. The rich man is a symbol of those
today who want to practice the ethic of crumbs. The ethic of
crumbs is a trickle down philosophy where the rich let the poor
have the leftovers so the latter could live just a little more com-
fortably. In a word, the ethic of the rich man who went to hell
is one of unrighteousness.

> When at holy communion we sing and pray 'let us break bread
> together on our knees,' we are not praying for an increased
> trickle of crumbs. We are praying for a relationship to God
> that compels us to do righteousness; that is, we are praying
> for a relationship to God that compels us to contribute to the
> empowerment of the people through sharing bread rather than
> crumbs.[26]

Christian theology is not only concerned with what is, but
with what shall be. To clarify how the present economic system and social condition are marked by chaos rather than community, and to speak of the church's stewardship of reconciliation, are existential aspects of theology. An existential theology critiques and analyzes the social plight of humanity in light
of God's revelation for wholeness and solidarity. In terms of
economic justice it addresses the problem of sin (i.e., greed,
idolatry, covetousness) and how sin alienates us from God and
each other. It looks at the nature and mission of the church as
a vehicle for salvation and social justice, and raises the issue of
whether the church remains a spiritual movement or becomes
just another institution in society.

From the other side of this issue concerning economic justice, theology deals with the question of what shall be. This

question is grounded in the idea of Christian hope and God's ultimate vision for a new community. In the eighth century, the prophet Isaiah was dealing with the question, "What shall be?" when he declared,

> and many people shall go and say, come ye, and let us go up to the house of the God of Jacob; and he will teach us of his ways, and we will walk in his paths: for out of Zion shall go forth the law, and the word of the Lord from Jerusalem. And he shall judge among the nations, and shall rebuke many people: and they shall beat their swords into plowshares, and their spears into pruninghooks: nation shall not lift up sword against nation, neither shall they learn war anymore. Isaiah 2: 3-4

In the book of Romans, the Apostle Paul addresses the question, "What shall be?" in a theological manner by saying "For we are saved by hope: but hope that is seen is not hope: for what a man seeth, why doth he yet hope for? But if we hope for that we see not, then do we with patience wait for it" (Romans 8:24-25).

No one person in the twentieth century has given more theological expression to the question of "What shall be?" than Martin Luther King, Jr. Dr. King addressed the question of "What is?" but he also addressed the question of "What shall be?" in his vision of what he called the beloved community. The vision of the beloved community was Dr. King's theological conception of God's new community in the world. It was a vision that demanded a new social order where people of different ethnic backgrounds would live together in brotherhood and share equally from God's resources. This vision spoke of breaking down the walls of segregation and discrimination, eradicating the sickness of racism and prejudice, and restructuring the economic system of our country so that poverty would no longer victimize certain people of our society.

This vision of the beloved community is important as it

relates to economic justice. Dr. King did not believe the vision could come to pass while economic injustice remained a reality in the society. Kenneth L. Smith and Ira G. Zepp, Jr. in their book, *Search for the Beloved Community: The Thinking of Martin Luther King, Jr.*, speak of Dr. King's emphasis for economic justice.

> King's views on economic justice and its importance for an inclusive human community reflect an early and consistent concern of King for an equalitarian, socialistic approach to wealth and property. A "life," he wrote, is sacred. 'Property is intended to serve life, and no matter how much we surround it with rights and respect, it has no personal being. It is part of the earth man walks on; it is not man.' King frequently chastised the United States for its economic system which withheld the necessities of life from the masses while allowing luxuries to be monopolized by the few. He believed fervently that one of the major goals of the United States should be to bridge the gap between abject poverty and inordinate wealth. The Beloved Community, in King's mind, would be a manifestation of God's intention that everyone should have the physical and spiritual necessities of life. To this end, during the latter part of his life, he began to advocate a variety of economic programs, including the creation of jobs by government and the institution of a guaranteed annual minimal income.[27]

Dr. King's vision of the beloved community was influenced by the teachings of Jesus Christ and the Christian faith. His vision was also influenced by Karl Marx, but his vision was not a communist concept. Throughout his life, Dr. King's messages and speeches were grounded in 'God talk.' His stand for a new economic order and social justice was another prophetic voice, just like Amos, Micah, and Isaiah who all spoke about justice, mercy, and peace. The vision of the beloved community beheld a future world characterized by economic equality.

> The dream is one of equality, of opportunity, of privilege and property widely distributed; a dream of a land where men will not take necessities from the many to give luxuries to the few; a dream of a land where men do not argue that the color of a man's skin determines the content of his character; a dream of a place where all our gifts and resources are held not for ourselves alone but as instruments of service for the rest of humanity; the dream of a country where every man will respect the dignity and worth of all human personality, and men will dare to live together as brothers.... Whenever it is fulfilled, we will emerge from the bleak and desolate midnight of man's inhumanity to man into the bright and glowing daybreak of freedom and justice for all of God's children.[28]

At a banquet at the Hyatt Regency Hotel in Louisville, Kentucky, I heard Mr. John M. Cramor III, President and Chief Executive Officer of Kentucky Fried Chicken, Inc., speak about "virtual reality." Virtual reality is an experiment in computer technology where a person can experience a reality, in some sense, before or without being there. We could call it technological empathy.

In actual reality, however, can you feel the way another person feels without having ever been in his/her position? Can you climb into another person's skin? We have our eyes and our ears. We can see and hear the hurts of the disinherited and oppressed. Sharing the American dream requires social and economic justice. It demands working toward God's desire for solidarity and community.

31

CHAPTER 2

A Historical Overview of Economic Justice and the Black Church

The quest for liberation and social justice has always been an intrinsic part of the life and ministry of the Black Liberation church. The pilgrimage of African American people has been a constant struggle against the evil of racism that perpetuates dehumanization and disfranchisement. As such, the Black Liberation church has historically served as a place of refuge and strength to a people who were forced to live in hostile conditions. Joseph R. Washington, Jr. spoke of this truth in the 1960's when he observed:

> Born in slavery, weaned in segregation and reared in discrimination, the religion of the Negro folk [chose] to bear the roles of both protest and relief. Thus, the uniqueness of black religion is the racial bond which seeks to risk its life for the elusive but ultimate goal of freedom and equality by means of protest and action. It does so through the only avenues to which its members have always been permitted a measure of access, religious convocations in the fields or in houses of worship.[29]

Because of the suffering and servitude that Black people

had to endure during the days of slavery, the Black Liberation church developed from her birth a different perspective of ministry than the White church. Gayraud S. Wilmore is correct in stating that,

.... from the beginning the religion of the descendants of the Africans who were brought to the Western world as slaves has been something less and something more than what is generally regarded as Christianity.[30]

The slave system perpetuated against Black people was a systematic effort to destroy the African family in relationship to its cultural identity, including religion. Contrary to the belief that African people were barbaric and had no knowledge of God, we know that the African people who were brought to America through the "middle passage" may have been forced to come with empty hands, but they did not come with empty heads, or hearts. The African slaves brought with them a rich cultural and religious heritage. All of the indoctrination, whippings, and other brutal efforts of the slavemaster to destroy the African slave's sense of culture and religious background failed.

Before the first organized Black churches were developed there was a Black Liberation church on the plantation which Black scholars refer to as "the invisible institution." The first generation of African priests served as preachers and counselors to the people. As preachers, they kept alive the religious instruction and theology of African culture. In the secret worship services, the African slave was strengthened mentally, emotionally, and spiritually. It was in the worship experience of the "invisible institution" that the slaves' culture, self-worth, and justice were kept intact, and where the spirit of insurrection was often developed.

Gayraud S. Wilmore speaks of the reality of the "invisible institution" and the spiritual integrity and sense of justice it infused into the hearts and minds of the African slaves.

34

The slaves were uneducated, by Western standards, but they were by no means ignorant. Almost immediately they recognized the gross inconsistency between the allegation that this all-powerful God of the whites could care so much about their eternal salvation while remaining indifferent to the powerlessness and wretchedness of their condition. Even though they adopted the outward appearance of Christian conversion, they took from it only what proved efficacious for easing the burden of their captivity and gave little attention to the rest. They were aware that the God who demanded their devotion, and from whom came the spirit that infused their secret meetings and possessed their souls and bodies in the ecstasy of worship, was not the God of the slavemaster, with his whip and gun, nor the God of the plantation preacher, with his segregated services and injunctions to servility and blind obedience.[31]

C. Eric Lincoln states that,

the Atlantic slave trade and the institution of slavery in the United States were rooted in the pursuit of economic gain. The Africans were pursued, purchased, and enslaved solely for the cheap labor they could provide on farms and plantations. They were the economic tools for the system of chattel slavery that reduced human beings to forms of property.[32]

From the atrocious days of slavery until the Civil War the majority of Black people in America were slaves. These slaves were made to live under a system designed to keep them in a "survival" context. The slaves had to depend on the plantation owner for the basic necessities of life: food, clothing, and shelter. Because the slaves were forced to undergird the American economy with free labor, White America got rich from Black peoples' blood, sweat, and tears.

Toward the end of the Civil War, there was a consciousness that the American society needed to be reconstructed. With this understanding the U.S. Congress, edged on by self-determined African Americans like Frederick Douglass, helped in the implementation of three Constitutional Amendments and a host of other laws. These changes were designed to create an avenue for the social betterment of African American people. In the early stages of this redistribution of social and economic power, the federal government (through the Freedman's Bureau) initiated a program of allocating abandoned land in the former Confederate states to the freedman in forty acre plots.

Lerone Bennett, Jr. gives support to this historical fact in his book, *Before The Mayflower: A History of Black America,* by stating:

> It was against this background, and in this spirit, that African-Americans began their march down the long road called freedom. That road branched off almost immediately into a swamp of racism and bad faith. We see this most clearly perhaps in the national reaction to the freedman's petitions for land. Some foreseeing politicians supported these petitions, saying that the freedmen were entitled, as a matter of justice, to retributive compensation for their 250 years of unrequited toil. Retributive was a big word to the freedmen; all they wanted was a little back pay. They saw what only the wisest saw: that freedom was not free without an economic foundation.[33]

However, this worthy vision did not live long. By 1865, the Freedman's Bureau was ordered to stop its land redistribution program. The failure of this land reform act and the failure of the Freedman's Bank in 1874 created a climate for social and economic impoverishment among African Americans.

Thus, African Americans began a long struggle against the social ills of segregation and disfranchisement empty handed.

It was against this kind of dehumanizing social setting that the Black Liberation church developed its economic ethic, which C. Eric Lincoln refers to as "the Black self-help tradition and the survival and liberation strategies." The economic ethic of the Black Liberation church has always consisted of a dualistic strategy of survival and liberation. The Black Liberation church saw the survival strategy as a means of helping one another to cope with the day-to-day traumas. The liberation strategy of this economic ethic was an expression of self-help designed to forge out a future in what looked like a hopeless situation. This economic ethic continues to be a part of the life and ministry of the Black Liberation church.

> The Black church is a reflexive institution that moves constantly between the poles of survival and economic arenas. On one hand, for its own economic survival, it is an institution that has taken part in the financial and economic transactions of the larger society and it has largely accepted capitalism as an economic system. On the other hand, the Black Church is the most economically independent institutional sector in the Black community. It does not depend upon White trustees to raise funds, for example, as do most of the Black colleges. Nor does it depend upon White patronage to pay its pastors or erect its buildings.[34]

In 1907 a conference was held at Atlanta University on "Economic Cooperation Among Negro Americans." W. E. B. DuBois noted that a historical sketch of cooperation among Negro Americans begins with the Black church. Because the Black Liberation church grew out of the crucible of slavery and was the primary institution that continued to carry the cultural, religious, and social teachings of the African past, the

37

Black Liberation church became the center of economic, educational, and social activity.

It was in the Black church that the insurrection movements for the freedom of African slaves had their origin. These insurrection movements are significant because in many instances they were carefully planned efforts at widespread cooperation for freedom. These cooperative efforts would eventually lead to peaceful economic cooperation. Among other scholars W.E.B. DuBois says,

> It was the fact that the Negro church thus loaned itself to insurrection and plot that led to its partial suppression and careful oversight in the latter part of the seventeenth and again in the eighteenth and early nineteenth centuries. Nevertheless, there arose out of the church in the latter part of the eighteenth and early in the nineteenth centuries the beneficial society, a small and usually clandestine organization for burying the dead; this development usually took place in cities. From the beneficial society arose naturally after emancipation the other cooperative movements: secret societies, and cemeteries which began to be bought and arranged for very early in the history of the church.[35]

The Black church, along with the mutual aid societies and the fraternal lodges, helped to create an economic atmosphere that suggested upward mobility and self-help. Such principles as thrift, industry, long-term investment, and personal discipline were advocated under this economic ethos. In 1887 there was not a single Black-owned bank, but by 1908, fifty-five banks had been started by Black churches or clergymen. Lerone Bennett, Jr. wrote,

> Supported by the bridges of the church, mutual aid societies and the fraternal orders, black businessmen moved in

the 1880's to a new ledge of economic activity, organiz-
ing the first black banks and the first black insurance
companies. The first black-owned banks were organized
in 1888, fifteen years after the Freedman's Bank de-
bacle.... There is a close connection between the found-
ing of these banks and the fraternal orders and the black
church. The True Reformers Bank was an organ of the
True Reformers, which was organized in 1881 by a
former slave, the Reverend William Washington Browne.
The Reverend W. R. Pettiford, pastor of the Sixteenth
Street Baptist Church, was the organizer and first president of the Alabama Penny Savings Bank.[36]

Because liberation and social justice are integral to the life
and ministry of the Black Liberation church, economic empowerment is addressed and practiced in a variety of ways. It
would not be unusual in the Black Liberation church, which
sees itself as an extended family, to help pay the rent or light
and gas bill for a parishioner who experienced an economic
crisis. Many young men and women have received significant
educational scholarships from their churches. Entrepreneurs
often receive financial support from members of their congregations. One of the dynamics of the Black Liberation church
experience is that of fellowship. After the worship service has
concluded and the benediction given, people do not leave immediately. People usually stay around, sharing with one another, sometimes as long as forty-five minutes. This period of
fellowship has provided Black people one of the most positive
atmospheres for marketing and networking their businesses.

Perhaps one of the most visible expressions of economic
empowerment from the Black Liberation church has been the
voice of protest it has raised on behalf of those who have no

voice. In a society marked by racism and social injustice, there are those who find themselves excluded from the mainstream of the market place. These people, who are mere statistics in society, receive help from the Black Liberation church, which has provided a collective voice of protest for the voiceless. A primary example of this is the role the Black Liberation church played during the civil rights movement. Dr. Otis Moss says,

> ...the Black church also provided social unity. It has provided limited educational support. It has provided a meaningful spiritual legacy. The thrust for freedom by Black Americans has found a home in the Black church. Please remember that our mass meetings were not held in a cathedral or a synagogue. You remind some people of that. The operational base for Dr. Martin Luther King, Jr. was the Black church.[37]

In his book, *The Social Teaching of the Black Churches*, Peter J. Paris accurately analyzes the Black church's involvement in economic empowerment. According to Paris, economic empowerment in the Black church was directly related to educational and moral development. The Black church was a significant economic institution itself, and provided major support for other Black economic enterprises. But the Black church as a whole never gave Black economic development a high institutional priority. Historically the Black church took the position that educational advancement and civil rights must be in place before economic empowerment could become a reality.

> It was generally agreed among the black churches that the economic standing of the race was directly proportional to the level of educational and moral development. Hence they believed that improvement in the latter would result in a

corresponding improvement in the former. Although many black economic enterprises had their beginnings in the black churches, and although the churches themselves constituted major economic institutions, they never gave high institutional priority to black economic development. Hence the churches expended much less energy in that sphere of their life than in education, moral training, and civil rights. The reasons for this are certainly multiple, but a major one is that blacks viewed education and civil rights as necessary conditions for economic development.[38]

The Black Liberation church remains today the most pivotal institution in the Black community. It is this writer's perspective that the Black Liberation church should take more seriously the vision of Black economic development in high institutional manners. Community development corporations should be a part of its ministry of social and economic justice.

During the 1960's, Rev. Leon Sullivan, who was pastor of the Zion Baptist Church in Philadelphia then, gave us a marvelous example of this type of vision in the development of the Opportunities Industrialization Center (OIC). Because Rev. Sullivan had a desire to see economic justice become a reality for Black people in Philadelphia, he started a program at the Zion Church called the Selective Patronage Program. Through his leadership, Rev. Sullivan was able to get four hundred other pastors and churches to participate. The pastors urged their congregations to refuse to do business with companies that refused to employ Black people. Between 1959 and 1963, there were twenty-nine selective patronage campaigns. It was estimated that as a result of these campaigns, more than two thousand skilled jobs were opened for Black workers. In 1962, Rev. Leon Sullivan was asked by Dr. Martin Luther King, Jr. to come to Atlanta and share the vision of this program. As a result, "Operation Breadbasket" was developed in Atlanta and Chicago.

41

Rev. Sullivan said,

> ...it was not our intention to destroy a business, but only to awaken it and to get it on the right road as far as the employment of Black Americans was concerned. We believed in free enterprise! We had no desire to destroy it; we wanted to strengthen it. But we wanted it strong for everybody, so that instead of the Black man getting the crumbs all the time, he would start baking some of the bread.[39]

Although the Selective Patronage Program had been successful, an onslaught of job opportunities was met by an unskilled Black labor force. The Opportunities Industrialization Center was born out of the need to train Black people for meaningful employment. The Office of Economic Opportunity had not come into existence, and the Department of Labor did not have Black people on their agenda. O.I.C. was successful because it was initiated by Black people, and addressed the real needs of people who had been shut out of the system for so many years. Some of the first courses offered in this program were drafting, sheet metal work, chemical laboratory technician training, power machine operating, and electronics assembly.

Another program Rev. Leon Sullivan developed to complement O.I.C. was the "10-36" plan. The purpose of this plan was to continue the process of economic emancipation. Although this was not an effort to nationalize Black dollars and labor, there was an understanding that if Black people were going to experience economic emancipation, they must have some sense of economic self-sufficiency.

Rev. Sullivan led a number of people in his congregation to pool ten dollars a month for a thirty-six month period. It was understood that the ten dollar participation for the first sixteen months would go toward education and scholarship benefits for children. The contributions of the final twenty months would be placed into investment corporations for profit making purposes. There were other Black churches that eventually participated in the plan. As a result of the "10-36" plan, an apartment complex called Zion Gardens was built, Progress Plaza Shopping Center, the first and largest black-owned and operated shopping complex in the United States was developed, and Zion Non-profit Charitable Trust was established, which used grants to provide other programs and human services for the disadvantaged.

Another pioneer in the area of church programs for economic empowerment was Rev. William Holmes Borders, who served as pastor of Wheat Street Baptist Church in Atlanta, Georgia. More than forty years ago Rev. Borders was leading the Wheat Street Baptist Church in ministries for economic development. The Wheat Street Baptist Church was one of the first churches in the nation to take the initiative to build affordable housing in the Black community. Through ministries of economic empowerment, this church has invested more than $15 million worth of development in its community. A 496-unit apartment complex, a 14-story development for senior citizens, and two neighborhood shopping centers have been built as a result.

For several years, Rev. W. N. Daniels has lead the Antioch Baptist Church in Chicago, Illinois, in ministries of economic development. A notable example of their commitment to economic liberation was the development of a project called the "Haven Homes." A four block area in the Englewood neighborhood was marked by decay and economic deprivation, but this church renovated this four block area into a 230-unit housing complex.

In more recent years, Black churches have continued their thrust for economic justice through housing developments, credit unions, nursing homes, schools, and business developments.

The Allen Temple Baptist Church in Oakland, California operates one of the strongest church-based credit unions in the country. The Corinthian Baptist Church in Dayton, Ohio has been empowering the Black community for several years through its credit union under the leadership of Dr. Perry E. Henderson. The Hartford Memorial Baptist Church in Detroit, Michigan has a multiplicity of economic empowering ministries. Some of these ministries include an auto shop, a 460-pupil school, and a $2 million credit union. New Zion Baptist Church in Louisville, Kentucky operates the 117-bed Intermediate Health Care Center in the Black community. The Allen A.M.E. Church in Jamaica, New York is bringing economic empowerment to its community by operating a 480-pupil elementary school, a health service facility, and a home care agency for the elderly and handicapped.

Through the years, the Black Liberation church has understood its ministry to include both evangelization and emancipation. The gospel preached in the Black Liberation church is centered around the theme of liberation. This gospel emphasizes the idea that God is concerned about the total person. In addition to the Black Non-Liberation church's belief that we only ought to get people ready for heaven, the Black Liberation church also believes we ought to empower people to live on earth.

The contemporary Black church is perhaps one of the most viable institutions in the African American community because it is the most independent institution that Black people own and operate. Civil rights organizations have played a significant role in the freedom movement of Black people, and are still needed today as an advocate for the oppressed. However, they are often limited in their ability to protest or represent the disinherited because of their funding sources. You cannot speak out against "The system" that you depend on to keep you alive.

Professional Black athletes and entertainers have access to

great financial resources that could benefit the African American community, and some noteworthy contributions have been made. But the limitations of this scenario is that apart from the Black Liberation church, there is no organizational structure that provides for ongoing investments into programs that can build our community.

The Black Liberation church has historically been on the vanguard for social and economic justice. As we move toward the twenty first century, we must continue to allow the Spirit of God to lead us in visions of liberation to set the captives free.

CHAPTER 3

Revolutionary Strategies for Economic Empowerment

The idea of revolution has been a constant theme in the life of the oppressed and those who fight for the liberation of the disadvantaged. To speak of revolution or revolt is considered by many people radical language and activity. These terms still carry negative connotations in our society. When the idea of revolution is expressed, there is the tendency to think in terms of negativism, destruction, killing, peacebreakers, animosity, and confusion.

However, when the idea of revolution is understood as a vehicle for social change to build and empower the lives of people who have been socially, politically, and economically deprived, it then conveys a positive and purposeful meaning.

Revolution, in a Christian sense, is the end of something, the fulfillment of something, and the beginning of something. If you want to examine the validity of any revolution from a Christian perspective, you must raise these questions: To what does the revolution bring an end? What does the revolution fulfill? What does the revolution begin?[40]

47

The Constitution of the United States declares, "We hold these truths to be self-evident that all men are created equal; that they are endowed by their Creator with certain inalienable rights; that among these are life, liberty, and the pursuit of happiness." But this American dream has been realized by only a few. A minority of people live in abundant wealth, while a majority of people live in degrading poverty. Those who live in abundant wealth become disturbed when those who live in degrading poverty speak of revolution and social change because it upsets the status quo. Those who live in degrading poverty are like Ralph Ellison's *Invisible Man*; they exist but others refuse to see them.

> I am an invisible man. No, I am not a spook like those who haunted Edgar Allan Poe; nor am I one of your Hollywood-movie ectoplasms. I am a man of substance, of flesh and bone, fiber and liquids and I might even be said to possess a mind. I am invisible, understand, simply because people refuse to see me.[41]

William A. Jones, Jr. says that a basic understanding of the spirit of revolution was given by Aristotle in his *Politics*. The chief cause of a revolutionary feeling is grounded in the desire for equality. The revolutionary spirit is freed when men of little means see and believe themselves to be equal to those who have more.

> The revolutionary spirit is rooted in the desire to be free, to experience and to enjoy equity, and it is grounded in certain ineluctable urgings of the human spirit. Men bound by oppressive brethren cry out, 'I want to be free. Something deep, down within me - that mysterious something called the soul - prods and pushes me, and demands of me that I break out of any unjust confinement to which sinful mortals subject me. Something good and Godlike in me rebels and revolts against

48

any and all forms of tyranny.' Regardless of any derogatory interpretation given to the revolutionary spirit by the elite, a genuine thrust toward personhood and or peoplehood should be regarded as sacred. Victims of tyranny who refuse to acknowledge and actively work for the fulfillment of their God-intended destiny as real persons do violence to the sanctity of their own creation.[42]

Another term closely related to the idea of revolution and social change is transformation.

> Transformation is a concept that permeates the biblical record from the Old Testament images of shalom and the reign of God in Israel to the New Testament church and the kingdom of God.[43]

Personal sin and institutionalized sin have distorted God's original design and purpose for creation. Racism, alienation, exploitation, oppression, and social injustice are visible manifestations of how sin has tainted God's created order. Transformation is God's continuing activity in history to restore and redeem a broken humanity.

From a theological perspective, the Christian community understands transformation to be at the heart of her mission and purpose for being. The Christian community is to serve as a co-laborer with God in transforming the world from a place of oppressive alienation to liberating solidarity. Paul says God has committed to the Christian community the ministry of reconciliation. Wayne G. Bragg suggests that,

> Transformation is a joint enterprise between God and humanity in history, not just a mechanistic or naturalistic process. It involves a transformation of the human condition, human relationships, and whole societies. The so-called 'developed' modernized world needs transformation to free itself from a secular, materialistic condition marked by broken relation-

ships, violence, economic subjugation, and devastation of nature; and the 'underdeveloped' world needs transformation from the subhuman condition of poverty, premature death, hunger, exposure, oppression, disease, and fear.[44]

The ideas of revolution, social change, and transformation were clearly a part of the life and ministry of Jesus Christ. Jesus Christ was a social activist. He had an agenda for the oppressed. Jesus is presented in many Christian communities as one who is confined to changing human hearts only. The gospels, however, present Jesus as one who is concerned about changing both human hearts and society as a whole.

When Jesus heals the lame man who had been sick for thirty-eight years at the pool in Bethesda, he is not only concerned about the condition of the lame man, he is also concerned about the condition of a society that cared more for inhuman laws than for human needs. When Jesus meets a man named Legion who is disturbed in his mind and ostracized from society, Jesus is not only concerned about Legion's mental healing, he is also concerned about changing the attitude of a society that can be comfortable with alienation.

Vishal Mangalwadi suggests that, Christ's compassion was a prophetic compassion. It was much more than a gut-level reaction as we would respond to pictures of starving children. Rather it was a compassion that grew out of a prophetic insight into the social and theological causes of suffering. Thus in his response, Jesus went to the root of human misery and dealt with it directly.[45]

The ideas of revolution, social change and transformation have characterized the social existence of African American people in America since the days of slavery. The struggle for freedom, civil rights, and human rights has kept the Black community in a revolutionary posture. From a religious perspective the Black community has been empowered to fight for freedom and social justice because the Black church understands God to be a redeemer who is concerned about total liberation. The Black Liberation church believes God wants us to minister to people in a wholistic manner, which would include dealing with social and economic justice.

In his book, *Prophesy Deliverance: An Afro-American Revolutionary Christianity*, Cornel West speaks of the value of prophetic Christianity. Prophetic Christianity is revolutionary in its practice in that it declares the right of every individual, regardless of class, country, race, or sex, to reach his/her potentialities. Prophetic Christianity says that every person has the right to experience what it means to be truly human. As a practice of social change, prophetic Christianity seeks to transform a society that expresses economic exploitation and dehumanization. The social vision of prophetic Christianity includes both existential freedom and social freedom. Existential freedom speaks to the sustaining of life and ultimately being delivered from any form of bondage. Social freedom is the power to exercise self-realization and the right to participate in a democratic society.

Cornel West says this type of Christian thought has made two major contributions to the African American experience.

> First, it confronts candidly the tragic character of human history, ...Second, prophetic Afro-American Christian thought elevates the notion of struggle (against the odds), personal and collective, regulated by the norms of individuality and democracy to the highest priority.[46]

The Black community as a whole has never accepted a fatalistic mentality. People of African descent have always lived with a sense of hope; we understand our potential for collective power.

> The simple presence of twenty-five million persons of African descent after centuries of maltreatment, miseducation, and ghetto misery says, clearly, that Blacks have not thrown in the towel. The sheer size of the Black population undercuts and vitiates the charge of total powerlessness.[47]

The visions of social change and constructive revolution have enabled the Black community to survive and to continue to struggle for justice and equality.

Theodore Walker, Jr. calls the importance of the church's involvement in economic empowerment programs the ethics of "breaking bread." Bread is a symbol for the various resources that provide for a wholesome social existence. The ethic of breaking bread is not concerned with paternalistic handouts or trickle down leftovers. The ethic of breaking bread is chiefly concerned with changing the conditions that create economic deprivation. According to Walker, both private and public sectors of society have a responsibility to participate in the ethics of breaking bread.

We do ourselves an injustice as a community if we fail to continue in the heritage of self-determination seeking to utilize our own resources for economic liberation. On this matter Walker raises a most insightful question: "What ought we African Americans in the U.S.A. do with the resources that we control in order to contribute to the comprehensive empowerment of all the people?"[48]

It is in response to this question that the Black community must grow and be strengthened in her efforts towards economic liberation. The problem has not been the absence of a vision, but rather choosing one to embrace. Another problem has been the mindset that we are a monolithic community.

There have been several visions of economic empowerment that have risen within the Black community. Every vision had its strengths and weaknesses, and every vision had a worthy contribution to make toward economic liberation. Although there were differences with each vision, there was a commonality among all the visions in that they all had the goal of economic empowerment for the Black community. As various visions for economic empowerment are presented today, the Black community must see the value in accepting the best aspects from a coalition of visions, rather than feeling a necessity to choose only one.

The visions of three prominent Black religious leaders—Malcolm X, Joseph H. Jackson, and Martin Luther King, Jr.—just recently impacted the Black community. The relatedness of their visions to the spirit of the Black Liberation church revolution make these men worthy of further study. These visions will be concisely presented in order to lift up the major elements of economic empowerment inherent in each and to emphasize the worthiness of a coalition of visions.

Malcolm Little was born in Omaha, Nebraska in 1925. The early days of his life were very distraught as he saw his family harassed by White racists. In Detroit, Michigan, Malcolm Little became known as Detroit Red, a known drug dealer and street hustler. This activity ultimately landed him in the Concord State Prison in Massachusetts. In prison, Malcolm became a student of Elijah Muhammad and embraced the religion of Islam.

Robert Michael Franklin is correct when he says of Malcolm X that,

> No major leader of the twentieth century was better acquainted with the deprivations, seductive pleasures, and repressed potential of ghetto life. As a consequence of this first-hand knowledge, he had an uncanny ability to diagnose the wounded psyche of the urban African American. Having diagnosed it with wit, guile, charm, and gusto, he aimed the awesome forces of his mind and voice toward the urban underclass to mobilize fellow wounded souls to claim their personhood.[49]

Malcolm X believed that Black people should develop the power to control their own destiny in America. He believed in the philosophy of Black nationalism, which advocated that Blacks should control the political, economic, and social institutions in their communities.

> Black nationalism refers to a body of social thought, attitudes, and actions ranging from simple expressions of ethnocentrism and racial solidarity to the comprehensive and sophisticated ideologies of Pan-Africanism as espoused by DuBois. Black nationalism is a complex ideological construct incorporating political, cultural, territorial, economic, and religious factors.[50]

From his religious convictions and philosophy of Black nationalism, Malcolm's vision for economic empowerment could be termed as community economic self-determination. Malcolm's basic position was influenced by Elijah Muhammad's ten-point "Muslim Program." In his book, *Liberating Visions: Human Fulfillment And Social Justice in African American Thought*, Robert Michael Franklin refers to three points of Muhammad's ten-point "Muslim Program" that places economic empowerment in the context of slavery and legally sanctioned discrimination.

> #4 We want our people in America whose parents or grandparents were descendants from slaves, to be allowed to establish a separate state or territory of their own - either on this continent or elsewhere. We believe that our former slave masters are obligated to provide such land and that the area must be fertile and minerally rich.

> #7 As long as we are not allowed to establish a state or territory of our own, we demand not only equal justice under the laws of the United States, but equal employment opportunities NOW!

#8 We want the government of the United States to exempt our people from ALL taxation as long as we are deprived of equal justice under the laws of the land.[51]

The acquisition of land was a key aspect in the Muslim's economic vision. With voluntary separation from Whites, they believed that Black people could develop their own form of self-government, economic self-reliance, and institutions that could build and strengthen their own community.

After his trip to Mecca, Malcolm X developed his own political organization known as the Organization of Afro-American Unity. For the remainder of his life, Malcolm emphasized the need of Black people to control their own destinies. As such, he was very concerned about the problem of poverty. Peter J. Paris states that Malcolm "viewed poverty among Blacks as an inevitable outcome of racism and poverty among the darker peoples of the world as the result of racism's twin, colonialism."[52]

Malcolm X believed that economic empowerment was intrinsically related to the overall freedom of Black people in America.

Economic exploitation in the Afro-American community is the most vicious form practiced on any people in America: twice as much rent for rat-infested, roach-crawling, rotting tenements; the Afro-American pays more for food, clothing, insurance rates and so forth. The Organization of Afro-American Unity will wage an unrelenting struggle against these evils in our community. There will be organizers to work with the people to solve these problems, and start a housing self-improvement program. We proposed to support rent strikes and other activities designed to better the community.[53]

55

In essence Malcolm X encouraged Black people to give themselves to self-development. Black people should develop and patronize their own businesses, thereby circulating their money in their own community.

The Rev. Joseph H. Jackson served as pastor of the historic Olivet Baptist Church in Chicago, Illinois. In 1953 he became president of the National Baptist Convention, U.S.A., Incorporated, and remained in office until 1982. Rev. Jackson is important to this study of economic empowerment because of his long tenure as president of the largest Black religious organization in America. As president of the National Baptist Convention, U.S.A., Inc., Rev. Jackson presented a vision of economic empowerment that certainly influenced other Black churches across the country.

Rev. Joseph H. Jackson was considered by many as a very conservative leader, a capitalist, and American patriot. Jackson did not believe that such practices as civil disobedience and protest were sufficient strategies for economic empowerment by themselves. His understanding of the person and ministry of Jesus Christ led him to take the position that all of our efforts toward economic and social justice must ultimately lead us toward the idea of community.

In *Black Religious Leaders: Conflict In Unity*, Peter J. Paris states that,

> Throughout Jackson's writings about the Christian faith there is an unmistakable implication that those who are faithful to Christ's ministry do, in fact, participate in the building of the kingdom of God. Since they must strive for the realization of that ideal in their historical period, it follows that the task of Christians in any society is to make that society the beloved community of God.[54]

As an American patriot, Rev. Jackson believed in the good

of America. He viewed the Constitution of the United States and the Christian gospel as being very compatible. As such, Jackson perceived the idea of democracy and the system of capitalism as being a compatible system wherein the Black community could take her rightful place.

> One of Jackson's basic presuppositions was that Black people had the ability to do much more than they were doing on every level of life. He proposed that Blacks build and rebuild their communities with such excellence that Whites might envy them and desire to move in.[55]

Jackson acknowledged the gains that had been won for the Black community through protest and demonstration. But he took the position that as Black people continued to struggle for justice (especially economic justice), the day was over for protest. It was time, according to Jackson, to move from protest to production. He felt that the Black community could not afford to continue to place major attention on what Whites were not doing for the Black community. Rather, Black people should examine their own efforts and make full use of their own resources. It would not be wise, from Jackson's perspective, for the Black community to remain primarily consumers; Black people must become producers to experience economic empowerment. In his book, *Unholy Shadows and Freedom's Holy Light*, Rev. Jackson gives a clear description of his economic philosophy.

> Protest has its place in the economic, political, and social struggle of mankind, and by it much good has been achieved. But I repeat, protest is not enough. We must go from protest to production. That is, we must seize every opportunity new and old in order to become creators as well as consumers of goods. We must become inventors as well as the users of the

tools of production and also the investors of capital as well as the spenders of it. Any Negro leader who shapes his philosophy, his theory and his practice as if the end of our economic struggle has been attained where we win the right to be hired in a factory owned by another is a traitor to the highest potentials of his race and a dangerous enemy to social progress, and a stumbling block to mankind. While we know employment is an economic necessity, earning and spending is not enough for a progressive people. After we have earned our money, there is no economic necessity laid upon us to spend it all within twenty-four hours for things that are not economically essential or morally sound. It is not wise to talk big and to spend big and then to save and invest little. We must learn how to organize our capital, harness our earnings and set them to work for us so that we may produce more and finally develop independent factories and companies of our own.[56]

The idea of self-development and self-reliance was intrinsic to the thinking of Rev. Jackson. Ironically, he could be associated with many Black nationalists. However, Jackson's emphasis on self-development and economic empowerment was centered around Black people receiving first-class citizenship and growing economically within the American system of capitalism.

Martin Luther King, Jr. was born and raised in Atlanta, Georgia in the home of a middle-class Black baptist family. He was formally educated at Morehouse College, Crozier Theological Seminary, and Boston University. The Christian nurturing and personal development he received at home, along with his educational training, prepared him to be an outstanding social prophet for the twentieth century. He is remembered and admired by people around the world for his leadership during the civil rights movement as an advocate for freedom and justice.

As a social prophet, King was very concerned about the problem of economic exploitation. "He advocated radical economic reform at a societal level and at the level of individual economic behavior."[57] King believed in the Protestant work ethic. He believed that individually we should see our financial responsibility as a sacred responsibility. He also advocated for a society whose economic system would eradicate the dualism of the "haves" and the "have nots." Martin Luther King, Jr.'s mission for economic empowerment was grounded in a vision he called the "beloved community."

King saw both systems of capitalism and communism as being inadequate for producing economic justice. He had lived in a society that practiced capitalism, and he had studied the social philosophy of Karl Marx. King's conclusion was that neither system was sufficient; what we needed was a synthesis of the two. Kenneth L. Smith and Ira G. Zepp, Jr. suggest that, though he never used the term, King's synthesis was a kind of "democratic socialism."

Communism failed to appreciate the value of individual expression and freedom. Communism's emphasis on the collective life created a society of coercing conformity. Capitalism failed to realize that the individual life is interrelated to the collective life. Capitalism, with its competitive behavior, creates an atmosphere where profit making becomes more important than human need. In his book, *Strength To Love*, King stated,

> We must honestly recognize that truth is not to be found either in traditional capitalism or in Marxism. Each represents a partial truth. Historically, capitalism failed to discern the truth in collective enterprise and Marxism failed to see the truth in individual enterprise. Nineteenth-century capitalism failed to appreciate that life is social and Marxism failed, and still fails, to see that life is individual and social. The Kingdom of God is neither the thesis of individual enterprise nor the antithesis of collective enterprise, but a synthesis which reconciles the truth of both.[58]

The vision of economic empowerment espoused by Martin Luther King, Jr. was centered around the immediate correction to the problem of Black unemployment, underemployment, and job discrimination. King placed strong emphasis on the role the federal government should play in eradicating the problem of poverty. In 1963, King proposed a "Bill of Rights for the Disadvantaged." This bill served the purpose of challenging the American government to utilize the resources of the society to work toward full employment.

Robert Michael Franklin states that the "Freedom Budget for All Americans," developed by the A. Philip Randolph Institute in 1967, was an economic plan for empowerment that King and the Southern Christian Leadership Conference fully embraced. Franklin identifies seven basic objectives proposed under this plan.

1. To provide full employment for all who are willing and able to work, including those who needed education or training to make them willing and able.

2. To assure decent and adequate wages to all who worked.

3. To assure a decent living standard to those who could or should not work.

4. To wipe out slum ghettos and provide decent homes for all Americans.

5. To provide decent medical care and adequate educational opportunities to all Americans, at a cost they could afford.

6. To purify our air and water and develop our transportation and natural resources on a scale suitable to our growing needs.

7. To unite sustained full employment with sustained full production and high economic growth.[59]

King was committed to a vision of economic empowerment as part of his stand for social justice. His radical economic plans and strategies of nonviolent direct action were designed to raise the consciousness of America about the problem of poverty and the sins of the nation. This was evident in the proposed plans he had for the Poor Peoples Campaign in Washington, DC.

Although these three Black religious leaders had different approaches in their vision for economic empowerment, the one commonality was that they were working for economic liberation on behalf of the Black community. Malcolm X believed in Black self-development through separation. Rev. Joseph H. Jackson believed in Black self-development through the system of capitalism. Rev. Martin Luther King, Jr. believed in economic justice through transforming government and other social institutions. There is a constructive aspect and an inter-relatedness with these visions. It is important for us to recognize the value of diversity in unity. A coalition of visions will enable the Black community to better address the multiplicity of issues related to economic justice, and it will enhance the spirit of collective economics.

The problems of economic and social injustice are the products produced by oppression. Mankind has the capability of practicing humanization or dehumanization. Humanization is the act whereby we seek to enhance the lives of others so they can experience what it means to be fully human. Dehumanization is the act whereby we seek to restrict the basic resources of life from others, thus reducing people to objects. The reality of oppression exists because too often people have chosen the practice of dehumanization.

If visions for economic empowerment are to be born and fully realized in the Black community, then there must be what Paulo Freire calls the "pedagogy of the oppressed." This is the process by which we educate people not to accept the conditions prescribed for them by others. Those who act as oppressors and practice economic exploitation want the oppressed to believe that they were created to live in ghettos, they are inherently limited in their intellectual capability, and their limited economic resources is due to their own laziness. When this perception of reality is accepted by the oppressed, they will exercise self-depreciation and oftentimes be fearful of the revolutionary ideas of freedom.

The pedagogy of the oppressed is the process of educating people to see for themselves that the oppressor's prescribed reality is a false reality. Therefore, the purpose of the pedagogy is not to take the oppressor's place, for the oppressor does not represent what it means to be fully human. This educational process is a vital part of any vision for economic empowerment because people in oppressive conditions must have their consciousness raised to fight for justice. It is not enough for leaders to have a consciousness for economic liberation. Freire states that,

> The correct method for revolutionary leadership to employ in the task of liberation is, therefore, not "libertarian propaganda." Nor can the leadership merely "implant" in the oppressed a belief in freedom, thus thinking to win their trust. The correct method lies in dialogue. The conviction of the oppressed that they must fight for their liberation is not a gift bestowed by the revolutionary leadership, but the result of their own *conscientizaceo*.[60]

As an educational process, the pedagogy of the oppressed is characterized by dialogue. According to Paulo Freire, true dialogue can only exist when the elements of a profound love for the world and man, faith in man's vocation to be more fully human, humility, hope, and the willingness to engage in critical thinking are present.

The Black Liberation church is one of the most viable institutions in the Black community for practicing the pedagogy of the oppressed. The themes of liberation and social justice have been and must continue to be a central part of the educational curriculum of the Black church. It is through educating people that we set the captives free.

CHAPTER 4

Case Studies: Religious Institutions with Ministries of Economic Empowerment

The history of the Black Liberation church authenticates it as the primary institution in the Black community that has fought for social change and economic justice. The Black Liberation church has always viewed its ministry as being wholistic. From the time of its inception to this present day, the Black Liberation church has sought to meet not only the spiritual needs, but also the social, economic, educational, and health needs of the Black community. Rebuilding the Black community and advocating economic self-help has always been on the Black Liberation church's agenda.

During the 1980's when Ronald Reagan's economic policy was forcing the poor "to make bricks without straw," an article was published in *Black Enterprise* entitled, "Churches Building Heaven on Earth: Rough times have spurred Black churches to new economic and political activism."

In this article, emphasis is placed on how many contemporary Black churches were adopting liberation theologies and ministries of economic empowerment to strengthen the Black community. Allen Temple Baptist Church, pastored by Dr. J. Alfred Smith in Oakland, California, was used as a primary example. This church sponsored the construction of housing, participated in building a small factory, and helped homeowners obtain rehabilitation loans to prevent gentrification in Oakland's Black community.

> "I preach a survival theology," said Dr. Smith. "I believe it is unethical to teach 'Thou must not steal' to someone who can't find a job. I know nothing about the furniture of Heaven or the temperature of Hell, but I do know about the urban wilderness."[61]

Author Elliott D. Lee concludes,

> Whether one calls it the wholistic gospel or survival theology, ministers like Smith are grappling with how the multi-billion-dollar Black church should best serve the bodies and souls of Black folk. No one knows for sure how much wealth Black churches possess or how much is used to improve the economic condition of their communities and the 20 million people who belong to their congregations. But history reveals a clear record of the Black church's involvement in economic development.[62]

In the *Detroit News and Free Press* (August 9, 1992), an article entitled "Who speaks for Black America?: Church, a force in rebuilding souls and cities" reported on the revitalization of an eight-block wasteland in the heart of one of Detroit's Black communities. Because of the vision of Dr. Charles G. Adams and the commitment of the congregation of Hartford Memorial Baptist Church, $1 million was invested to purchase the land in 1985. A McDonald's, Kentucky Fried Chicken and several small auto shops are now operating on this same eight-block area. What was once a wasteland is now a productive area, providing jobs and stability to a Black community.

Reporters Angelo B. Henderson and Janice Hayes state that,

> In Black communities across the United States, Black
> churches are doing more than singing the Lord's praises. They
> are taking on the economic, social and political issues plagu-
> ing Black Americans with the same vigor with which they
> confront the devil himself.[63]

It is believed that "Black churches take in at least $1.7 bil-
lion annually."[64] Combine that with the facilities and properties that many of these churches possess, and you have a pow-
erful institution for promoting economic empowerment in the
Black community. This realization is becoming more evident
since traditional civil rights organizations seemingly do not have
the same thrust and effectiveness they once had for social
change. According to C. Eric Lincoln in an article in the *Detroit News*, "The lack of an economic agenda has hurt traditional civil rights groups, and that's part of the reason the Black
church is seen as a more effective force in the community."[65]

CASE STUDIES

Nine Black religious institutions that presently have ministries of economic empowerment were studied by the author.
These churches range in size from very large congregations to
small. Their locations vary from urban to suburban. The
churches used in this study are affiliated with different denomi-
nations. The purpose of this case study is to examine what
types of ministries of economic empowerment are being imple-
mented, what difficulties are associated with the development
of this type of ministry, how viable these ministries are today
for social change, and what basic principles should be considered in the development of Canaan's Community Development
Corporation. A church questionnaire on economic empower-

ment ministries was designed as the instrument for conducting this case study.

Case #1   Antioch Baptist Church
East Chicago, Indiana

A.   AGE

The Antioch Baptist Church is seventy years old. It was organized in 1922 for the benefit of persons who held membership in First Baptist Church some distance away.

B.   ACTIVE MEMBERSHIP

The active membership of Antioch Baptist Church is 450. The congregation is very diversified between senior citizens, middle age, and youth. The same would be true of the economic status of congregation.

C.   LOCATION

Antioch Baptist Church is located in an inner-city/urban area.

D.   SOCIAL CONSCIOUSNESS

Antioch Baptist Church has a strong social consciousness through its study of biblical liberation motifs, African American history, and the Black presence in the Bible. The majority of the membership believe in the theology of dominion, that is, taking control of our spiritual, social, political, and economic destiny in the exercise of our Kingdom stewardship.

E.   MINISTRY OF ECONOMIC EMPOWERMENT

Antioch's ministry of economic empowerment is called the Antioch Baptist Progressive Associates. This organization is composed of members of Antioch Baptist Church and other individuals in the community who have united in a joint venture of saving and investing for the purpose of becoming economically empowered.

F.   SUPPORT BY GRANTS FOR BASIC OPERA-
     TIONAL

No. This ministry does not receive outside support in any form.

G.   KEY RESOURCES

Key resources include the number of participating members, amount of individual investment, the clarity of visions, the desire for economic empowerment, and bypassing the $50,000.00 cash reserves necessary to become an investment corporation.

H.   DIFFICULTIES

The process of economic empowerment is slow, and there is a need to maintain sufficient interest on the part of individuals who invest small accounts and look for large, immediate returns.

I.   IMPACT ON COMMUNITY AND CHURCH

The potential for impacting the community is tremendous, but has not yet materialized. Although there is no measurable impact on the community, there are measurable differences attitudinally within the church family. When the church provides leadership and structure for the personal and collective economic empowerment of the people, people begin to see the church in a different light.

J.   EVALUATIVE PROCESS

General evaluations are held through monthly meetings and advisory committees which include a basic evaluation of success or failure of investment.

K.   A COLLECTIVE EFFORT AMONG BLACK CHURCHES FOR ECONOMIC EMPOWERMENT

The need for churches in the African American community to come together for economic empowerment is great and the potential is even greater than immediately recognized. The churches in the African American community are the stewards of great economic empowerment, but the effort is poorly managed and given to others for safe-keeping and for their profit exclusively. Before large numbers of churches will come together in this kind of economic empowerment venture, fewer churches must work to develop successful models which can be easily replicated by others.

Case #2   First Institutional Baptist Church Phoenix, Arizona

A.   AGE

Founded in 1905, the First Institutional Baptist Church is eighty-seven years old.

B.   ACTIVE MEMBERSHIP

The active membership is approximately 1,500. The predominately middle-class African American congregation represents every age group.

C.   LOCATION

The church is located in an urban community. Many members live in the suburbs.

D.   SOCIAL CONSCIOUSNESS

First Institutional Baptist Church has an extremely strong social consciousness; this congregation has been a prophetic Christian witness in the Phoenix metropolitan area, the state, the nation and even the world for several years. Their theological basis is Luke 4:16-21.

E.   MINISTRY OF ECONOMIC EMPOWERMENT

First Institutional Baptist Church has several ministries of economic development. The Broadway House is an 80-unit low-income housing project. FIBCO Family Services, Inc. is a non-profit corporation which provides emergency shelter for the homeless. The First Institutional Workshop Program hires young people to work at the church for their first job experience. They are paid minimum wage. First Institutional has plans to form a corporation called FICRIC (First Institutional Community Reinvestment Corporation).

F.   SUPPORT BY GRANTS FOR BASIC OPERATIONAL EXPENSES

The church does not receive outside grants.

G.   KEY RESOURCES

Key resources for the implementation of this ministry is through tithes and offerings, and using the gifts and talents of our members.

H.   DIFFICULTIES

The major difficulty encountered has been getting enough committed people to engage their gifts and talents to the development of church programs.

I.   IMPACT ON COMMUNITY AND CHURCH

The impact on the community has been the implementation of wholistic assistance, and the impact on the church has been the development of an attitude of collective responsibility.

J.   EVALUATIVE PROCESS

General evaluations occur during quarterly church business meetings.

K.   A COLLECTIVE EFFORT AMONG BLACK CHURCHES FOR ECONOMIC EMPOWERMENT

There is a definite need and a possibility for churches in the Black community to come together for economic empowerment. We will need to remove petty parochialism and think about the greater needs of the people.

Case #3   Allen Temple Baptist Church
Oakland, California

A.   AGE

The Allen Temple Baptist Church is 73 years old. It was organized in 1919.

B.   ACTIVE MEMBERSHIP

The active membership is approximately 3,000. The middle-class African American congregation represents every age group.

C.   LOCATION

It is located in an inner-city/urban area.

D.   SOCIAL CONSCIOUSNESS

This congregation has a very strong social consciousness. It has been developed through preaching, teaching, and the pastoral ministry in community activities for social justice. Theologically these understandings are grounded in the gospel of Luke 4:16-21.

E.   MINISTRY OF ECONOMIC EMPOWERMENT

Allen Temple Baptist Church Federal Credit Union: cooperative association organized by Allen Temple church members in accordance with the provisions of the Federal Credit Union Act. Its purpose is to promote thrift among its members and create a source of credit for provident and productive purposes. It is a viable Christian institution for members and their families, allowing them to become owners and shareholders of a bank.

F.   SUPPORT BY GRANTS FOR BASIC OPERATIONAL EXPENSES

No grants or funds are received from any outside entity. The Allen Temple Church at large is the sponsor of all programs, and provides initial capital. The church now provides office space and utility service.

G.   KEY RESOURCES

The National Credit Union Administration (NCUA) serves as a key resource for this congregation. State and Local Credit Union League chapters provide training and resource information. Church members and the community provide help as volunteers in certain specific areas.

H.   DIFFICULTIES

Difficulties have included the lack of experience in banking and credit union operation of its early founders, and overcoming limited faith and belief by many church members. Slow growth factor has impacted the number of services that can be offered matched by low priority by some church leaders, and a lack of commitment of volunteers.

I.   IMPACT ON COMMUNITY AND CHURCH

Community impact has been minimal so far. Future potential impact is awesome given the limited number of financial institutions located in our community. Impact on church: They have provided full or part-time employment for six church members. They have provided financing for several real estate acquisitions by the church, automobile financing and payroll deductions for members who are employed by the church, and a depository for church funds. The church members are beginning to show pride and confidence in their credit union by investing in a financial institution that actually belongs to them.

J.   EVALUATIVE PROCESS

The evaluative process for determining longevity of the Credit Union ministry is ongoing through consistent measurement of member growth to member needs. The financial strength and safety of the credit union is evaluated on a monthly basis by meetings of the board and in-house Supervisory Committee. The C. U. receives an annual examination by the National Credit Union Administration (NCUA), which determines the future viability of the credit union by rating in areas of management, liquidity, capital, and asset/liability management.

K.   A COLLECTIVE EFFORT AMONG BLACK CHURCHES FOR ECONOMIC EMPOWERMENT

Yes, there is a need for Black churches to work together for economic empowerment. We must overcome some barriers that hinder our cooperative spirit. But the possibility of building a coalition is certainly very viable. It must be done first on a small scale.

Case #4   Twelfth Street Missionary Baptist Church Detroit, Michigan

A.   AGE

The Twelfth Street Missionary Baptist Church was founded in 1944.

B.   ACTIVE MEMBERSHIP

The active membership is approximately 750. The average church member is thirty-eight years old. This is a middle-class African American congregation.

C.   LOCATION

The church is located in an inner-city/urban area.

D.   SOCIAL CONSCIOUSNESS

This congregation has a strong social consciousness. Theologically this consciousness has been developed through preaching, teaching, and community involvement. There is an emphasis on how we arrange our resources to glorify God and build the lives of people. Redemption is viewed in terms of ministering to people in a wholistic manner.

E.   MINISTRY OF ECONOMIC EMPOWERMENT

REACH, Inc. is a non-profit community development and service organization organized out of the "Weekday Ministry" of the Twelfth Street Missionary Baptist Church. It was established in 1986 to meet the socio-economic needs of the Pilgrim Village community. REACH provides a wholistic approach to community development in three broad areas: (1) Human Development, (2) Physical Development, and (3) Economic Development.

F.   SUPPORT BY GRANTS FOR BASIC OPERATIONAL EXPENSES

This ministry does receive grants. These grants have been from private foundations.

G. KEY RESOURCES

The most important resource is seen as the church family. The relationship the church has with the community is very essential. The knowledge base for developing this ministry is to be acknowledged in the resources people provide from the congregation.

H. DIFFICULTIES

The greatest difficulty is viewed as the misunderstanding that people have about the church. The idea that the church should not be involved in socio-economic issues must be dismissed.

I. IMPACT ON COMMUNITY AND CHURCH

The ministry has had a tremendous impact on the community. Neighborhoods that were destroyed by drugs have been reclaimed and drug dealers have been forced to evacuate. There has been crime reduction and a new sense of pride in the community. The impact on the church is that it has forced the church to move to a new level of ministry. The involvement in the community has increased the growth of the congregation and demanded a change in the development and implementation of existing ministries.

J. EVALUATIVE PROCESS

General evaluations are conducted during board meetings and special committees to determine the effectiveness of the ministry at present and its vision for the future.

K. A COLLECTIVE EFFORT AMONG BLACK CHURCHES FOR ECONOMIC EMPOWERMENT

There is a definite need for Black churches to work together for economic empowerment. There are barriers to overcome, but the possibility is certainly a worthy goal. It must first take place on a small scale. This will provide a model for greater involvement.

Case #5   Brown Memorial Church
Louisville, Kentucky

A. AGE

The Brown Memorial Church is 138 years old.

B. ACTIVE MEMBERSHIP

The active membership is approximately 588. The average age within the congregation is 58-60. The majority of the congregation is professional/educated, and low to moderate income.

C. LOCATION

The church is located in the urban area of the city.

D. SOCIAL CONSCIOUSNESS

The Brown Memorial Church has a strong social consciousness. The theological basis for what they believe and practice as a local congregation is grounded in the social creed of the Christian Methodist Episcopal Church under the caption "Theological Perspective."

We believe that the Christian Methodist Episcopal Church is a part of the body of Christ, and that it must express itself in the world in the light of the life and teachings of Jesus Christ. Jesus taught us many things both by word and example - to be concerned for the welfare and the well-being of others, to love our neighbors as ourselves, and to be concerned about justice. For the church to be silent in the face of need, injustice, and exploitation is to deny the Lord of the church. We believe out of one blood God made all the nations that dwell on the face of the earth, that Jesus is most uniquely His so that all men are brothers and each person is of infinite worth, and a child of God. Thus, pride, or arrogance is thoroughly unbiblical and un-Christian.

E.   MINISTRY OF ECONOMIC EMPOWERMENT

The ministry of economic empowerment that is functioning presently within the Church is called "Project One." The Brown Memorial CME Church, under the leadership of the Reverend Charles J. King, Jr., gave birth to this ministry in 1985 to help find summer jobs for economically disadvantaged youth in the Greater Louisville and Jefferson County communities. The Project One impetus stemmed from the thousands of teenagers and young adults who were denied work during the relatively idle summer months, but had no mechanism to get jobs from private sector companies.

F.   SUPPORT BY GRANTS FOR BASIC OPERATIONAL EXPENSES

This ministry has received financial support from local financial institutions and private sectors.

G. KEY RESOURCES

Leadership, pastoral freedom, collaboration with parents, schools and the business community are absolutely necessary for the success of the program.

H. DIFFICULTIES

The difficulties they have encountered in implementing ministries of economic empowerment are as follows:

(a) Insufficient capital
(b) Lack of volunteers
(c) Paper work/busy work

I. IMPACT ON COMMUNITY AND CHURCH

The impact Project One has had on the community is that it has assisted in building the job-readiness skills, basic skills, and self-esteem of over 1,500 youth who have successfully completed the program and were placed in meaningful jobs at participating corporations. Church members learned that they must do more than tithe; they must be involved in the process of economic development for our youth and young adults.

J. EVALUATIVE PROCESS

A committee of volunteers from the private and public sectors meet to determine how successfully the program's objectives have been met. Youth employers also provide quantitative data to show the effectiveness of the training and highlight key factors in success of the program. Also, areas of improvement are discussed to strengthen the service delivery of the program, goals and objectives.

K. A COLLECTIVE EFFORT AMONG BLACK CHURCHES FOR ECONOMIC EMPOWERMENT

Because social and economic injustice is still prevalent, the need and possibility for churches in the Black community to come together for economic empowerment is more necessary now than ever before.

Case #6 Monumental Baptist Church
Jersey City, New Jersey

A. AGE

The Monumental Baptist Church is 92 years old.

B. ACTIVE MEMBERSHIP

The active membership is approximately 3,000. The congregation consists primarily of young to middle age persons. The majority of these persons are professionals: salespersons, middle managers, small business owners, and other professionals.

C. LOCATION

This church is located in the heart of an urban setting.

D. SOCIAL CONSCIOUSNESS

The Monumental Church has a strong social consciousness. Theologically, this consciousness is based on the idea that God is interested in saving the whole person. Matthew Chapter 25 would be one of the biblical texts for undergirding this position. Through preaching, teaching, and involvement

79

in outreach ministries for the community, this congregation has come to realize that the church has more than a marginal relevancy. The ministry of Jesus Christ serves as an example that the church should be designing her ministry to serve people in a wholistic manner.

E.   MINISTRY OF ECONOMIC EMPOWERMENT

The Monumental Baptist Church has created a ministry of Business Development. The purpose of this ministry is to encourage and assist Black people to become entrepreneurs. Because the Monumental Church is located in the heart of an urban center, equipping persons to own their own business is a viable avenue for economic empowerment. Through the development of Black businesses, people have ownership in their community. Training on business development is provided by the church and a networking system has been designed to encourage support.

F.   SUPPORT BY GRANTS FOR BASIC OPERATIONAL EXPENSES

The Monumental Church takes pride that no outside sources finance any of their ministries or projects.

G.   KEY RESOURCES

The key resources for this ministry are as follows:

1. Support of the congregation
2. Leadership development
3. Awareness through education

H. DIFFICULTY

The difficulty in this type of ministry is the slow process that is involved. People have to be encouraged not to give up because they do not see immediate development. There is also the challenge of helping people change their negative attitudes, and to believe in themselves in spite of racist barriers.

I. IMPACT ON COMMUNITY AND CHURCH

The impact on the community is that people are seeing the church in a new light. The church is being viewed as a daily ministry and not a weekend affair. The community sees the church as being concerned about social, political, and economic issues. The impact on the church is that it has stimulated people to practice the principle of Christian stewardship. Members are able to help provide employment for other members.

J. EVALUATIVE PROCESS

General evaluations are conducted during quarterly church business meetings.

K. A COLLECTIVE EFFORT AMONG BLACK CHURCHES FOR ECONOMIC EMPOWERMENT

There is definitely a need for Black churches to develop a collective ministry for economic empowerment. For this to take place, a small scale model should be developed first. This model could provide the example and excitement for a national model.

81

Case #7 Allen A.M.E. Church
Jamaica, New York

A. AGE

The Allen A.M.E. Church was founded in 1834.

B. ACTIVE MEMBERSHIP

The active membership is approximately 6,000. This is a middle-class African American congregation.

C. LOCATION

This church is located in an inner-city/urban area.

D. SOCIAL CONSCIOUSNESS

This congregation has a strong social consciousness. Theologically this consciousness is centered on the ministry of Jesus Christ. Throughout his ministry, Jesus identified with the poor, oppressed, and disinherited. The members of the Allen A.M.E. Church believe they have been called to rebuild the community. Housing, education, and the development of jobs are the main focus of their ministry.

E. MINISTRY OF ECONOMIC EMPOWERMENT

Allen A.M.E. Church has several ministries of economic empowerment. They have a school, pre-kindergarten to eighth grade, that generates about $2 million and provides sixty jobs. The training of children is an economic investment. Allen Housing Development Corporation is a senior citizen housing complex. Allen Neighborhood Corporation builds homes and manages commercial properties. The purpose is to bring economic investment into the community, create jobs, and stabilize property values.

F.   SUPPORT BY GRANTS FOR BASIC OPERATIONAL EXPENSES

This ministry does receive federal and private grants.

G.   KEY RESOURCES

The key resources for this ministry of economic empowerment are as follows:

(1) Tithes and offerings
(2) Human resources
(3) Leadership development

H.   DIFFICULTIES

The difficulties encountered in implementing ministries of economic empowerment are as follows:

(1) Limited vision in leadership of congregation.

(2) The challenge of changing attitudes about the mission of the church.

(3) Educating people to understand the difference between investment and the leveraging of money.

I.   IMPACT ON COMMUNITY AND CHURCH

The impact on the community is that people see the church

as a servant of the community. These ministries have brought economic stability to the community and provided other avenues to receive needed support. The congregation feels a sense of fulfillment in knowing they have improved the quality of life for others. The church's evangelistic effort has also been raised. Ministries of economic empowerment attract people who want to be involved in pro-active ministry.

J.   EVALUATIVE PROCESS

General evaluations are conducted during quarterly church business meetings. There is an internal accounting process with a certified CPA.

K.   A COLLECTIVE EFFORT AMONG BLACK CHURCHES FOR ECONOMIC EMPOWERMENT

There is a need for Black churches to come together for economic empowerment. As we move toward the twenty first century, the Black community cannot look to government alone for a future; we must build our own. A small scale model should be developed first. This type of model could be replicated by churches across the country.

Case #8   The Shrine of the Black Madonna Detroit, Michigan

A.   AGE

The Shrine of the Black Madonna is about 44 years old. It was organized in 1950 by Albert B. Cleage.

B.   ACTIVE MEMBERSHIP

The active membership is approximately 500. The congregation represents persons of every age group.

C.   LOCATION

It is located in an inner-city/urban area.

D.   SOCIAL CONSCIOUSNESS

The congregation of the Shrine of the Black Madonna
has a very strong social consciousness. They understand their
mission to be that of building economic power, through educational and skill development. Theologically, they take the
position that Jesus Christ was concerned about the disinherited and downtrodden. Through preaching, teaching and practical programs, they have developed a belief that their calling
is to set the captives free.

E.   MINISTRY OF ECONOMIC EMPOWERMENT

The Shrine of the Black Madonna has developed a cultural center and book store for economic empowerment. There
are three centers: Atlanta, Houston, and Detroit. The cultural
center and bookstore were developed so that Black writers
and artists could have an outlet to share and market their works.
Presently, 6,000 book titles are in inventory. The profit from
the sale of books and art is reinvested to stock more African
American products. The center has been self-sufficient since
1975. The Shrine of the Black Madonna also has an apartment
complex which houses a community center. The apartment complex was acquired to house members of the Shrine. In this
center, computer classes are offered for children and adults.
They also provide a reading readiness program. The Shrine
of the Black Madonna is working on a vision called the Beulah
Land Project. They are seeking to buy 5,000 acres of land,
upon which they intend to grow food for the poor in our deprived communities. They also plan to build a campus on

this land where youth from the inner city, whose lives have been marked by trouble, will live and receive skills and education for redirecting their lives.

F. SUPPORT BY GRANTS FOR BASIC OPERATIONAL EXPENSES

They receive no grants; projects are supported totally by the congregation.

G. KEY RESOURCES

The most important resource is seen as the people who make up the congregation. The development of people is viewed as key to providing resources for community development.

H. DIFFICULTIES

The greatest difficulty is getting people to understand the vision. Limited resources and the time it takes for some visions to become a reality creates some sense of difficulty.

I. IMPACT ON COMMUNITY AND CHURCH

The Shrine finds difficulty in getting its message and mission over to the community. They would like to be a vital force in bringing economic empowerment to the African American community. The church members know they have improved the quality of life for themselves by pooling their resources and working together to build a stronger community.

J. EVALUATIVE PROCESS

General evaluations are held through board meetings and

special committees to determine the effectiveness of the ministry at present and its vision for the future.

K.   A COLLECTIVE EFFORT AMONG BLACK CHURCHES FOR ECONOMIC EMPOWERMENT

Although the Shrine understands the need for Black churches to work together for economic empowerment, they really do not see that as being possible.

Case #9   The Nation of Islam
Chicago, Illinois

A.   AGE

The Nation of Islam is sixty-four years old. It was established in 1930 by Master W. Fard Muhammad, who passed leadership on to Elijah Muhammad.

B.   ACTIVE MEMBERSHIP

The active membership is approximately 200,000 in more than 200 cities across the United States of America.

C.   LOCATION

Most chapter or mosque locations are in inner-city/urban areas.

D.   SOCIAL CONSCIOUSNESS

The Nation of Islam has a strong social consciousness. They understand their mission to be that of building economic power through educational and skill development. They believe that African Americans should unite to build a new

87

nation and separate from their oppressors. The Nation of Islam has a special prison ministry where the members teach African American inmates about their culture and history in order to free their minds from the misinformation they learned in the public schools that do not teach Africentric studies.

E.   MINISTRY OF ECONOMIC EMPOWERMENT

The Nation of Islam has its own university through which it teaches vocational and entrepreneurial skills. Its restaurant and bakery employs individuals who have successfully completed training in the various skill areas. The Nation also has its own publishing company that it uses to disseminate information about its programs and ministries. They have also been awarded million dollar contracts nationwide to provide security for housing developments, including the Chicago Housing Authority.

F.   SUPPORT BY GRANTS FOR BASIC OPERATIONAL EXPENSES

They receive no grants; projects are supported totally by their members, including the sale of their products and services.

G.   KEY RESOURCES

The most important resource is viewed as the sale of their newspaper, *The Final Call*. Also, the bakery sells thousands of bean pies weekly. The development of its members is the key to providing resources for community development.

H.   DIFFICULTIES

The greatest difficulty is viewed as getting many people to understand the vision. Many have limited the Nation of

Islam to being a hate group because of its teaching of self-love and Black pride.

I.   IMPACT ON COMMUNITY AND CHURCH

The impact on the community is that people see the Nation of Islam as a servant of the community. The Nation has used its own unarmed security force to clean up drug-ridden neighborhoods which has allowed many people to once again have a strong sense of pride in their neighborhood. Its ministries of economic empowerment have attracted many people who want to be involved in a pro-active ministry.

J.   EVALUATIVE PROCESS

General evaluations are held by special committees as determined by the National Head of the Nation of Islam, Minister Louis Farrakhan.

K.   A COLLECTIVE EFFORT AMONG BLACK
     CHURCHES FOR ECONOMIC EMPOWERMENT

Although the Nation of Islam sees the need to work together with all other Black religious institutions to bring economic empowerment to the African American community, it is not probable that many Christian churches would be willing to work with the Nation of Islam due to its non-belief in Christianity.

There are several other Black churches across the country that are involved in economic empowerment, including First A.M.E., Los Angeles, Pastor Chip Murray; St. Paul, Brooklyn, Dr. Johnny Youngblood; Trinity United Church of Christ, Chicago, Dr. Jeremiah A. Wright, Jr.; and St. Stephen Baptist Church, Louisville, Dr. Kevin Cosby.

✟   ✟   ✟

The Black church is still the primary institution that carries the hopes and aspirations of the Black community. No other institution, including the traditional civil rights organizations, have the following of Black people like the Black church. Because the Black church is the one institution that is owned and operated exclusively by Black people, it has the freedom prophetically to work for social justice.

Because our society is saturated with racism, sexism, and classism, social and economic injustice continues to characterize America. As such, the Black church must continue to strongly encourage the Black community to work for Black self-development and Black self-reliance. The Black church must remind the masses of Black people that there are some things Black people must do for themselves, or it will never be done.

Ministries of economic empowerment will continue to be a necessity as we move toward the twenty-first century. There are a variety of avenues a church can take in developing ministries of economic empowerment. A church should study the context in which it is doing ministry and develop its vision of economic empowerment based on the need of the community.

The size of a church's congregation does not determine its ability to implement a vision of economic empowerment. The commitment of a small congregation can give birth to this kind of ministry. The talents and skills of people are as valuable a resource for ministry as money. Ministries of economic empowerment take some time before they show major results; therefore, we must encourage people to practice patience.

It is imperative that we practice the pedagogy of the oppressed in developing a ministry of economic empowerment. Through the process of education, people are prepared to fight for economic justice. Through this process of education a church can be demythologized of myths that would hinder this kind of ministry. Consumer Education and Collective Economics should be seen as imperative aspects of the Black church's pedagogy of the oppressed.

Churches that are serious about economic empowerment must be careful of receiving grants from the federal government, or private foundations. An institution owned and operated exclusively by Black people, the Black church has enjoyed her freedom to be prophetic. A church must be careful not to let a grant silence the prophetic voice.

Ministries of economic empowerment help to build a sense of solidarity in the Black community. It is expressive of the African communal philosophy, "I am because we are, and since we are I am." It helps to remove the destructive Western philosophy of rugged individualism.

Churches that have ministries of economic empowerment gain a new respect from the community. The community views the church as having a daily agenda for the oppressed, as opposed to being seen as only a "Sunday situation."

Ministries of economic empowerment reflect an ongoing struggle, theologically and practically, in the Black church to ensure relevancy as we move toward the twenty-first century.

There is wide agreement among Black church leaders that there is a need for a coalition of Black churches to work together for economic empowerment. Perhaps the best starting place would be for a group of churches in a local community to collaborate on an economic development project. These models could then be replicated across the country.

Canaan Church is one of the strongest institutions in Louisville's African American community.

Financial planning was among the topics discussed in seminars for Canaan's members.

CHAPTER 5

Model of Ministry: Canaan's Community Development Corporation

Because of the economic condition of the Black community in Louisville, Kentucky, the Louisville Urban League, in conjunction with city government, initiated a program entitled "Goals for Greater Louisville." The program was designed to address the issue of economic growth in communities across the city. The Community Reinvestment Act has inspired some of the financial institutions in the city to do a better job in providing financial resources in the Black community for housing and business development.

In March 1992, I was invited by the Mayor to participate in a special task force to discuss and plan ways to bring economic investment into the Black community known as the West end. This task force was developed because the Mayor and other community leaders realized that the city of Louisville could not grow as a stable community if there continued to be economic development in the East end (White community) and economic deprivation in the West end (Black community).

The task force was made up of community leaders from across the city, including the directors of the Urban League, Community Action Agency, and Economic Development Office; representatives from financial institutions, Black business developers, city and state officials, and Black pastors all attended the meetings. The primary idea that we discussed was known as the "Development Bank Concept." This concept came from a project developed in Chicago's South Shore neighborhood.

Fifteen years ago the South Shore neighborhood in Chicago was infested with crime and drug abuse. Unemployment was prevalent and landlords were deserting their properties.

Today the neighborhood is stable and economically strong. New businesses have been started, people have received remedial education, and there is also job placement. Fifteen years ago the South Shore neighborhood was 99 percent Black, and today the community is still 99 percent Black.

As David Osborne states in an article entitled, "A Poverty Program That Works," the "program" is the Shorebank Corporation in Chicago's South Shore neighborhood. Shorebank is a holding company that includes a bank, a real estate development corporation, a small venture capital firm, and The Neighborhood Institute, an organization that develops low-income housing and provides remedial education and vocational training. Within a small circle of foundation, anti-poverty activists, Shorebank is legendary. In Washington, it is almost unknown. Yet it is the perfect model for the 1990's: inexpensive, market-oriented, and entrepreneurial.

The purpose of the task force was to discuss how this model could be replicated in Louisville, Kentucky. This experience was another confirmation for me of the importance of the Black church leading the Black community toward economic empowerment. One of the critical questions as it relates to the Development Bank Concept bringing economic investment into the West end was, What kind of ownership will the Black community have in this development?

The Black community will never experience true economic liberation and equality without having a sense of ownership. And so the question that confronts the Canaan Church and other Black churches as we move toward the twenty-first century is, How will we continue to enable the Black community to experience economic empowerment? In response to this question, we at the Canaan Missionary Baptist Church developed a model economic empowerment ministry.

The purpose of Canaan's Community Development Corporation is grounded in the idea of God's desire for justice and solidarity to exist among all people. As a non-profit organization, Canaan's Community Development Corporation will strive to change the social and economic conditions of the Black community in Louisville, through educational forums, scholarships, child development programs, building affordable housing, and other business initiatives.

The rationale of this ministry is that there are some things Black people must do for themselves or they will never get done. We believe in the concept of self-determination. Black self-determination is not grounded in the idea of humanism, the idea that mankind is sufficient in and of himself. Humanism seeks to turn men and women into gods.

Black self-determination involves the integrity and courage of Black people who persevere, even against the odds. It is Black people's refusal to allow their dignity and destiny to be determined by someone else. The idea of Black self-determination was born in the crucible of slavery where people of African decent came together to pray and plan for their future. V. P. Franklin, speaking of the challenge of Black self-determination, says that

> If the Afro-American nation in the United States is to move
> beyond its present condition of comparative economic inequal-
> ity and political subordination, the cultural vision of the

masses of Afro-Americans must be tied to a progressive economic program. That economic scheme must have the realization of each individual's potential and socioeconomic well-being, as well as the preservation of particular cultural perspectives and traditions, as its primary objectives. To date, Black and White capitalists (and the American capitalist system in general) have failed to accept the challenge of Black self-determination. Perhaps it is time that Afro-Americans began to pursue alternative economic visions for realizing their full social, political, and cultural potential in the United States.[66]

In the Gospel of John, there is the story of how Jesus took a little boy's lunch that consisted of only five barley loaves and two small fish and fed over five thousand people. The disciples wanted to send the people away because they saw themselves as poor and the little boy's lunch as insignificant. But Jesus understood the importance of using what you have, thus was able to feed the multitude with the little boy's lunch.

The Black community may have limited resources, but they can make a difference. Through the practice of individual stewardship and collective economics, we can prepare the Black community for economic empowerment. In an article entitled, "Blacks should use their billions to call their own shots," Barbara Reynolds reminds us that,

> much is written about Black poverty, but taken as a group, Blacks aren't poor. They earn about $300 billion yearly and buy 50% of all movie tickets. More than 54% own bank cards, says Exit Travel Magazine. If Black wealth were well-organized and leveraged, it could reap huge payoffs. About 1 million Blacks attend national or regional conventions or reunions yearly, spending about $16 billion on airplane tickets, hotels, car rental, clothes and baby sitters. If Black groups would set aside $3 billion of what is spent at conventions, the interest on it would be $400 million.[67]

Like Jesus, we must recognize the importance of using what you have.

Our goals included:

1. Educating people on the economic principles that govern our country, and the role the church must take to help work for economic justice.

2. Developing a financial system so that Canaan's Community Development Corporation can be self-sufficient, that is, independent of grants or loans from financial institutions or the Federal Government.

3. Implementing a partnership with major financial institutions and other organizations of good will in the city for community development projects.

4. Raising the consciousness of the congregation to the need for ministries that address the struggle for economic and social justice.

5. Establishing seed money for educational scholarships for youth.

6. Assisting people in the development of a business through a basic entrepreneurial training program.

7. Fostering a stronger sense of economic cooperation and solidarity in the African American community.

Canaan's Community Development Corporation was designed as a non-profit, non-stock corporation under and pursuant to the laws of the Commonwealth of Kentucky. Canaan's Community Development Corporation is a separate legal entity.

Canaan's Community Development Corporation is a non-member corporation. The only members of the corporation are the Board of Directors. The corporation was designed as such in order to protect it as a ministry of the church. If the corporation had been designed as a membership corporation, then people across the city who have no affiliation with the church or understanding of the corporation as a ministry of economic empowerment could join, possibly taking the corporation away from its original purpose and rationale.

The Board of Directors is made up of seven persons. The Initial Directors will serve for a three-year period. The purpose of the Initial Directors is to lay the foundation— adopt the organization's rules and by-laws, and establish policies to manage the day-to-day operations. The Initial Directors also have the responsibility for hiring the Executive Director of the corporation.

Seven persons were chosen from the congregation of the Canaan Church to serve as the Initial Directors. The seven directors consist of four men and three women. The occupational backgrounds of the directors are as follows: Marketing Manager, Real Estate Developer, Commercial Lender, Business Entrepreneur, Health Care Worker, Office Manager, and Distribution Manager.

The permanent Board of Directors will be elected as follows: Upon the expiration of the terms of the Initial Directors, six of the successors will be elected at the annual congregational meeting of the members of the Canaan Missionary Baptist Church. Also, at the annual meeting, Director seven will be appointed to serve as Chairman of the Board of Directors by the Trustees and Deacons of the Canaan Missionary Baptist Church. Each Director will serve a term of one year.

The Officers of the Corporation include a Chairman of the Board, a Vice-Chairman of the Board, a Secretary, and a Treasurer.

The Board of Directors employ the Executive Director who serves as the Chief Operating Officer of the corporation. The Executive Director gives general supervision, direction, and control of the business of the Corporation. Although the Board of Directors constitute the only membership of the corporation, the congregation of the Canaan Church has ownership in the Corporation. The congregation of the Canaan Church determines who serves on the Board of Directors annually, and the Chairman of the Board is appointed by the trustees and deacons of the church. As such, the congregation of the Canaan Church has a viable influence on the direction of the Corporation. Because Canaan's Community Development Corporation is understood as a ministry of the Canaan Church, the Board of Directors makes a report to the church at our quarterly church mission meetings.

One of the most important aspects in the development and design of Canaan's Community Development Corporation was the preparation of the Board of Directors. There is a difference between the design and purpose of the Canaan's Community Development Corporation (C.C.D.C.) at the Canaan Church and the Community Development Corporation (C.D.C.) that functions at a financial institution. Unlike a church ministry, they operate solely as "corporations" emphasizing development primarily as a business transaction. The funding for these Community Development Corporations comes primarily from outside sources.

The Community Development Corporation at the Canaan Church is more than a corporation; it is a ministry of economic empowerment. The primary financial support for this ministry does not come from any outside source. The Community Development Corporation of the Canaan Church is rooted in God's redemptive purposes whereby people are liberated (even economically), to experience what it means to be truly human. As a ministry of the church, the final accountability is to God.

The preparation of the Board of Directors was presented in two parts. The following issues were explored:

Part I

   A. Community Development Corporations - what are they, what purposes they serve

   B. Non-profit, non-stock corporations

   C. The officers of the corporation and their function

   D. The purpose of Canaan's Community Development Corporation

   E. The by-laws were explained and developed.

   F. 501(c)(3) organizations

Part II

   A. The church's theology

   B. The history of the Black church and economic justice

   C. Christian stewardship and community outreach

   D. How and why this corporation is a ministry of the Canaan Church

   E. The importance of congregational involvement and ownership

   F. How this ministry of economic empowerment relates to the church's vision for the twenty-first century

100

In the previous chapter, the case studies showed how independent churches must be careful of receiving grants from the federal government and private foundations. We decided that we did not want any outside financial support to restrict the church's prophetic voice. Therefore, the primary financial support for this ministry comes from the Canaan Church.

Because of the strong emphasis at the Canaan Church on Christian stewardship, we decided the best way to develop a systematic financial support for Canaan's Community Development Corporation would be through our giving on Sunday morning. We also decided to ask the congregation to make their contribution through a special fund to the church, and then let the church make the contribution to Canaan's Community Development Corporation. This means our financial support continues to give emphasis on the corporation as a ministry of the Canaan Church. It also provides an opportunity for the church to express her commitment to building the community, and for the community to recognize the support of the church.

A special offering envelope was designed for the congregation to support this ministry entitled, "Canaan's Community Self Help Fund." Everyone is encouraged to give $5 each week to this fund. We do not have any rich people in our congregation, but most people can afford to give $5. Five dollars may seem insignificant by itself, but when given by a collective body, it can make a great difference. For example, if three hundred people give $5 every Sunday, by the end of a year, seventy-eight thousand dollars ($78,000) would be contributed to the cause of economic empowerment.

Through the practice of Christian stewardship, we are providing regular financial support to this ministry of economic empowerment. Because we are building for ourselves a stable financial foundation, whenever the Corporation seeks partnership with other institutions, we will be seen as builders and not beggars.

In order to raise the consciousness of the congregation for support of this ministry, we felt it necessary to market this ministry in the church. Marketing a new ministry allows the church family to become familiar with it, as well as create a sense of excitement about its value in the life of the church and community.

One avenue used for marketing this ministry was the use of flyers in the Sunday morning worship program. Because of the regular attendance of people at Sunday worship, this is prime time to give visibility to this ministry. We also sent letters to every family in the church explaining to them the purpose of Canaan's Community Development Corporation and how this new ministry would impact the community.

Another major marketing avenue for gathering the support of the congregation for this ministry was networking through our Congregational Care Ministry. As lay ministers work with the families in their care, they are able to make personal contacts encouraging people to support Canaan's Community Development Corporation.

A dramatic presentation entitled "When The Table Turns" was presented at a congregational fellowship dinner to emphasize the importance of our support to this ministry of economic empowerment, and the difference it can make in the lives of people. This drama was based on the story in Luke 16:19-31 about the rich man who refused to share his resources with a beggar named Lazarus. A contemporary situation was presented to show how we would respond to Lazarus today. The question raised was, What kind of personal and collective response will the church make to Lazarus as we move toward the twenty-first century?

Through our marketing efforts, we were able to raise the congregation's awareness and enthusiasm for this ministry.

CANAAN'S COMMUNITY DEVELOPMENT CORPORATION: PROJECTS

A. EIGHT-WEEK EDUCATIONAL FORUM ON ECONOMIC JUSTICE

The first project initiated by Canaan's Community Development Corporation was an eight-week educational forum on economic justice. The purpose of this educational forum was to raise the consciousness of the congregation regarding the need to establish ministries of economic empowerment. Paulo Freire's concept of the pedagogy of the oppressed was instrumental in this effort.

This educational forum was held for two hours on Thursday evening from 6:00-8:00 p.m. The average attendance was about sixty people. The audience was made up of adults of all ages. The largest representative group was middle-age adults. The following are the eight sessions that were presented:

Session I. **Principles of Biblical Stewardship: Individual Responsibility**

The word stewardship comes from the Hebrew word (steward) *stigweard*. *Stig* means house or household, and *weard* means keeper. The connotation of the two words together is of a steward who is a keeper or overseer of a household or an estate. For Christians, stewardship is the recognition of God's ownership over one's person, powers, and possessions, as well as the faithful use of these for the advancement of Christ's kingdom in this world.

In Genesis 1:28 we are told,

> And God blessed them, and God said unto them, Be fruitful, and multiply, and replenish the earth, and subdue it: and have

dominion over the fish of the sea, and over the fowl of the air, and over every living thing that moveth upon the earth.

Within this verse are two phrases which speak to us about God's intention for christian stewardship: "Subdue it" and have "dominion over." God wants us "to take charge." God wants us to possess things. God does not want things to possess us.

Of all the possessions that people are allowed in this life, money is one area that seems to plague us the most. However, money is neither good nor evil. It is neither moral nor immoral; money is amoral. It is capable of good or evil, depending on the use made of it. The test of money is the use of money. Therefore, the use one makes of money is dependent on one's attitude toward money.

Tithing is the minimum standard of Christian giving. Just as the Jews were mandated to tithe under Mosaic law, Christians are spiritually moved to give not less than one-tenth of our earnings when we consider the example of Christ in the giving of his life. The following scriptures were shared to provide further clarification:

    (1) Leviticus 27:30-33 (the Lord's tithe)
    (2) Numbers 18:21-24 (the Levite's tithe)
    (3) Deuteronomy 14:22-27 (the festival tithe)
    (4) Deuteronomy 14:28-27 (the poor tithe)
    (5) Malachi 3:8-10
    (6) Genesis 14:18-20
    (7) Genesis 28:20-22
    (8) Proverbs 3:9-10
    (9) Matthew 23:23
    (10) Luke 21:1-4

The emphasis of this session was that we must be responsible persons with the financial resources God has provided us within support of the ministry of the church.

Session II. **Principles of Biblical Stewardship:**
Collective Responsibility

The church is the body of Christ and Christ is head of the body. Oftentimes, we have been engaged in the collective work of the church even though we may not have recognized it as the body of Christ. The personalization of religion is not something that is inherent within Black people. This emphasis has been handed over to us by the dominant religious culture. Many of the hymns we sing ignore the collective aspect of our faith.

Because of this unbalanced emphasis on individualized religion, we often have difficulty embracing the church as a collective body. Good religion is both personal and collective.

Once we understand that as a church we are the collective body of Christ, we must ask ourselves what it means in terms of our ministry in the world. In I Corinthians 16:1-2, Paul says to the Church at Corinth,

> Now concerning the collection for the saints, as I have given order to the churches of Galatia, even so do ye. Upon the first day of the week let every one of you lay by him in store, as God hath prospered him, that there be no gatherings when I come.

Paul is asking a church as a collective body to be responsible in their stewardship.

The church is a non-profit business. The church is seeking to respond to human need. As such the church will always need financial support to carry out its ministries. The church can give dignity to the idea of stewardship by being responsible as a collective body. Through the years churches have used different methods to gather financial support for its work.

1. Taxation - State churches in Europe were tax supported.

2. Commercialism - an example of this would be bake sales.

3. Begging - an example of this would be baby contests.

4. Biblical Stewardship - teaching people to give their tithe and offering out of love and a sense of responsibility to God.

After receiving financial support through the practice of individual stewardship, the church as a collective body must practice responsible stewardship through ministering to human need. The "Great Commission" in the gospel of Matthew 28:19-20 speaks of the mandate given to the church to minister to the world. It is through our togetherness or collective responsibility that we can carry out this task.

As the church gives financial support to local associations and national conventions for the work of missions, then the local church can minister around the world. In II Corinthians 5:17, we are told, "Therefore if any man be in Christ, he is a new creature: old things are passed away; behold, all things are become new." As new creatures in Christ, we receive a new perspective on life. Part of that new perspective is a concern for others.

When it comes to the African American community, the Black Liberation church is still the strongest institution we have. Since the Black Liberation church is the centerpiece of the Black community, it assumes a heavy responsibility. The Black Liberation church carries the hopes and aspirations of a new day. The Black Liberation church must continue to reach out to the Black community as a collective body ministering to human needs and empowering the lives of people.

The New Zion Baptist Church, under the leadership of Dr. A. Russell Awkard, has a sense of collective responsibility. This congregation has sponsored the James S. Taylor Nursing Home. It is the only Black-owned and operated nursing home in the state of Kentucky. It ministers to the needs of elderly and indigent people in the Black community.

The emphasis of this session was that the church has a stewardship to fulfill as a collective body. The church is called to serve God and to serve people. The Black church must see social justice as part of its stewardship responsibility.

Session III. A History of the Black Church and Economic Justice

In this session particular notice was given to how the Black church has historically been on the vanguard for social and economic justice for the Black community. An explanation was given of how the Black church developed a theology of hope and a spirit of Black self-determination during the dark days of slavery.

The problems African Americans faced economically after the Emancipation Proclamation and the role the Black church played were underscored. W.E.B. Dubois said that economic cooperation among Black people began in the Black church. In both the Baptist and Methodist churches, there was the vision of developing economic ministries that would enhance the lives of Black people. These economic ministries were called mutual aid societies.

An early prototype was the Free African Society developed by Richard Allen and Absalom Jones. The Wheat Street Baptist Church developed similar societies called the Rising Star and the Sisters of Love. It was because of this type of economic cooperation in the Black church that several Black insurance companies got their start.

Attention was given to how Black churches in recent years have continued to work for economic justice. The development of the Opportunity Industrialization Center by Dr. Leon Sullivan at the Zion Baptist Church in Philadelphia was used as a primary example. (A full description of what was covered in this session is presented in Chapter IV, A History of the Black Church and Economic Justice.)

The emphasis of this session was to remind the congregation of the Black church's rich heritage in its fight for the liberation of the African American community. The audience was encouraged to consider new visions of economic empowerment so our ministries remain relevant as we move toward the twenty-first century.

Session IV. <u>Idea of Community in the Biblical Tradition</u>

The Bible presents us with the unfolding drama of God's purpose being fulfilled. We can see this unfolding in the covenant made with Abraham, the Red Sea episode, and the covenant established at Mount Sinai. The major thematic thread running through each of these mighty acts of God is the purpose of developing a special community of people who willingly participate and accept their relationship with God, and maintain a just relationship with others.

Equally clear is the purpose for which God calls the church to work for community. The community is not mythical; it is reality within time. But the community is also eschatological; it has a futuristic aspect about it. In essence, the community is the Kingdom of God, and it will be fully realized in the eschaton, or "end time." God's ultimate purpose is the actualization of the kingdom, but that will take place in the "end time." And so the question is, what do we do in the meantime?

In the meantime, the church is called to create a new community in the world. In Genesis 12:1-4, God tells Abraham that through his seed every family of the earth will be blessed. Abraham is remembered for his faith in responding to God's call to establish a new community. Likewise, the church today cannot respond rightly to the challenge of creating community in a world marked by chaos unless we have a real and substantive faith in God.

The story in the book of Exodus 14:13-16 of the children of Israel being delivered from Pharoah through the Red Sea reveals again God's progressive move toward the establishment of a new community. This story certainly symbolized what God would ultimately do for humanity through Jesus Christ. In the land of Egypt, the children of Israel were slaves. They were dehumanized in every conceivable manner. But God delivered them so they could experience what it means to be truly human and experience a new kind of community with one another. No one should allow himself/herself today to be a slave to anyone except the Lord Jesus Christ. In our salvation experience God delivers us not only from personal sins, but also from institutional sin.

At Mount Sinai, God gave clarity to Israel's call to establish community.

> Now therefore, if ye will obey my voice indeed, and keep my covenant, then ye shall be a peculiar treasure unto me above all people; for all the earth is mine: And ye shall be unto me a kingdom of 144 priests, and a holy nation. These are the words which thou shalt speak unto the children of Israel. Exodus 19:5-6

Israel knew how to be a crowd, but they did not know how to be a community. The law was given to Israel to guide them in establishing community. Instead of reaching out to others in community, Israel was content to keep God to its self.

The problem today in the Black community is that some people have lost their sense of collective consciousness, and brought into the Black churches the Western idea of rugged individualism. But if there is going to be the establishment of real community, then rugged individualism has to be supplanted.

The early church in the Book of Acts provides an outstanding paradigm for how the church today should express community.

> Then they that gladly received his word were baptized: and the same day there were added unto them about three thousand souls. And they continued steadfastly in the apostles' doctrine and fellowship, and in breaking of bread, and in prayers. Acts 2:41-42

The fellowship of the early church was marked by a genuine concern for others. The call of the church to build community cannot be complete without a proper devotion to God. Our call to build community has both a horizontal and vertical dimension. Unlike the early church, the contemporary church too often diminishes the meaning of fellowship to simply eating together. But breaking bread in the New Testament day was expressive of a bonding taking place between persons.

The emphasis of this session was to help persons understand what community means from a biblical perspective. Our call to establish community should move us to reach out into the community in ministry.

Session V. Black Theology and Humanization

Education leads people out to a new perspective on life. Black theology is an important part of Black church life because it provides a wholistic framework within which to understand the social crises of our day.

Theology involves the struggle of every person to understand God's movement in the world and in his/her life. Black theology is Black people understanding God through the lenses of their own perspective. Theology is never created in a vacuum; it is always shaped and developed out of one's social context. Therefore, Black theology raises the question, What does it mean to be Black and Christian?

There is a growing awareness today that the issues of Black poverty, unemployment, and political alienation are not separate from the theological concerns of the church. These realities are theological issues about which the church should be concerned. We need to be engaged more in the thinking of how God is involved in the collective struggle of our liberation. This kind of critical thinking should then be incarnated into practical ministries of empowerment. Without an adequate theology of our own, we will borrow the theology of someone else. When we do this, we continue to participate in our own dehumanization and exploitation. It is time for the Black church to become responsible for its own theological thinking. For the Black church's understanding of the meaning of God is just as credible as any other theology.

Dehumanization is the process of treating people as less than full human beings. Systems and institutions that practice dehumanization take away from us the dimension of self-understanding. If the Christian faith means anything it means we learn how to be human under the freedom of God. Being dehumanized by social structures is still very much a part of the struggle of the Black community. It is the particular responsibility of the Black church and Black theologians to articulate an understanding of God that frees us from such exploitation.

Unfortunately the understanding of Black theology is not known in many Black churches. In some cases, the term would be viewed as being radical. But Black theology has always been a part of the Black church experience. We must continue

111

to emphasize the truth that no one can speak of our experience with God for us, or better than us. What we have to say about God as Black people is liberating, and it creates an ethic for justice with which the world ought to grapple. From the days of slavery, Black people have been grappling theologically with what it means to be fully human under the freedom of God. Black theology came into being as a corrective to the narrowness and non-liberating understanding of God's redemptive involvement in the history of oppressed people. It was a protest against the dehumanization of Black people that was accepted by the White church and its theologians. It was a response to the White church that had nothing to say about God's liberation for an oppressed people.

The gospel of Jesus Christ has more to say to us than just living a virtuous life. Every Sunday Black people who are poor and hurting come to our churches wanting to know if God has an agenda for the oppressed. The essence of the gospel is about liberation, justice, and the kingdom of God bringing people to a wholistic understanding of themselves in relationship to God.

As Black theology continues to address the problem of dehumanization, it must do so both structurally and personally. Black people experience dehumanization from many different angles. The negative images of Black people on television, the ghettoizing of Black life, and economic exploitation are all examples of dehumanization. Therefore, as we continue to strive to be fully human under the freedom of God theologically and practically, we must address the problem of daily pain and the system that perpetuates the pain.

The emphasis of this session was to recognize how Black theology has enabled us to grapple with the problem of dehumanization, and to help the congregation realize that liberation must be on the agenda of the Black church if we are going to experience what it means to be fully human.

Session VI. Budgeting and Money Management

Budgeting as it relates to money management was the focus of this session. Three different budgets were presented to the group to show the importance of consumer education at every age level, and for different situations.

1. Children
2. Single
3. Married

It is vital that we teach our children economics and consumer education at an early age. Consumer education should also be viewed as part of the church's economic empowerment ministry. It was pointed out that weekly allowances and games such as monopoly provide an excellent opportunity for this kind of education. Youth ministries within our churches should view economics as part of the wholistic nurturing of our children in the faith.

In the presentations made concerning the operation of budgets with adults, the following general principles were encouraged:

1. Every person should practice the principle of tithing, as it is part of being a responsible christian.

2. If renting or buying a house, one should not pay more than 28 percent of the gross income.

3. One's car payment should be no more than 10 percent of the gross income

4. We should pay ourselves 10 percent of gross income. Tithe 10 percent, save at least 10 percent, and live on the 80 percent.

113

5. It is important to do a quarterly or yearly economic projection.

6. One should learn to live within his/her economic boundaries. Being thrifty is a good practice.

7. The use of credit cards should be avoided because of high interest rates.

8. One should make economic plans for retirement as soon as possible, and study the different investment vehicles available for accomplishing this goal.

9. When operating a budget, one should develop short and long-range financial goals, and recognize the difference between fixed and variable expenses.

10. Discipline is required for operating a budget.

The emphasis of this session was to stress the importance of money management. To show how the use of operating a budget can aid one in being a better steward.

Session VII. <u>**The Black Church and Economic Strategies**</u>

The story of the children of Israel's bondage in Exodus 3:7-4:5 provides us with parallels and principles akin to the predicament of Black America. There are two general strategies in this story for economic and social justice. Moses is sent by God to tell Pharoah "to let my people go." An appeal is made to Pharoah to act justly. This strategy entails a prophetic call to justice. The Black church must continue to cry out with a prophetic voice asking government and corporate institutions to have just and humane policies, and to provide economic opportunities and relief for those who have been denied.

The second general strategy is that Moses and the children of Israel were not to depend on Pharoah for what they could do for themselves with the help of God. The second strategy speaks to the importance of self-help.

It is important for people who are living in oppressive conditions to have a faith that allows them to see both the negative and positive implications of their plight. Pharoah's meanness demanded of the children of Israel a stronger sense of community, and recognition of the resources that God had already provided for them. Moses did not think much of the rod in his hand, but it was in an oppressive condition that he realized his rod was a tool for liberation. The Black community should not see its economic condition as a problem, but an opportunity.

Four approaches for implementing a strategy of self-help are as follows:

(a) Band-Aid Approach - Some social theorists would not advocate this approach. However, the Band-Aid Approach is necessary because it deals with survival. Sometimes we have to treat symptoms before we can deal with the case. The Band-Aid Approach does not solve the problem. This approach would include feeding the hungry, clothing the naked, and providing shelter for the homeless.

(b) Correlated Approach - This approach focuses on the alleviation of issues that have a relatedness to economic oppression. For example a person who has a drug addiction can potentially be very employable. Therefore, dealing with the issue of drugs is correlated to the liberation process of economic empowerment. Educational and job training programs would be a part of this approach.

(c) <u>Direct Cure Approach</u> - This approach speaks of the importance of direct personal involvement in the healing ministry of economic empowerment. It means that Black people must personally support Black business. The practice of Christian stewardship both individually and collectively as a church would be a part of this approach.

(d) <u>Spiritual Maintenance</u> - In our effort to lead people out of oppressive conditions and to empower them economically, it is important that we nurture their lives in Jesus Christ. Spiritual maturity is the foundation for preparing people for liberation. Discipleship training is part of this approach.

The emphasis of the session was to understand the bases of developing strategies for economic empowerment.

Session VIII. <u>Canaan's Community Development Corporation</u>

The purpose of this seminar was to inform the congregation how Canaan's Community Development Corporation would function as a ministry of the Canaan Church, and how this ministry would help bring economic empowerment to the Black community.

The seminar was presented as a two-part presentation. Part I was centered around a videotaped television interview on economic empowerment in the Black community. Two Black ministers, Rev A. Russell Awkard, pastor of the New Zion Baptist Church, and the author, were invited to speak on *Close Up*, a local talk show program concerning economic empowerment in the Black community.

The pastors were asked, such questions as:

How are your churches involved in economic empowerment?

Is there a sense of pride in the Black community for revitalization?

How do you respond to the idea that affirmative action is rediscrimination?

Do Black people who experience upward mobility feel a sense of responsibility for helping other Black people move up?

What part does the Federal Government play in helping to bring social and economic empowerment to the Black community?

Is there any correlation between what Canaan's Community Development Corporation is planning to do and what Leon Sullivan and O.I.C. did during the 60's?

What kind of financial strategy will the church use to support the Canaan's Community Development Corporation, or where is the capital coming from?

The first thirty minutes of the seminar was used to view this video on economic empowerment. Following the video was a questions and answers session.

In general, the congregation commented that the Black church has always been involved in social and economic justice. However, as we move toward the twenty-first century, the Black church must make its presence felt stronger in these areas because of the setbacks Black people have experienced in recent years. The importance of community was shared. The congregation felt that the Black community did not have the sense of oneness it should have. Too many people have accepted the Western philosophy of rugged individualism. The Black church must help the Black community and the community at large to understand our accountability to God and our responsibility to each other. In response to the question concerning the role of Federal Government in helping to bring social and economic empowerment to the Black community, it was stated that the Federal Government could be a facilitator. The Federal Government could provide more financial support for worthy programs instead of responding after a crisis has developed. Regarding the idea of affirmative action being reverse discrimination, several persons voiced the fact that affirmative action was one of the opportunities for White America to try and balance the scales of equality, and that America is still far behind in the redistribution of social and economic opportunity.

During the second half of the seminar, a lecture was given on the purpose and operations of Canaan's Community Development Corporation.

The goal of helping to bring economic empowerment and development to the Black community will be achieved through the following avenues:

1. Educational Forums
2. Church Family Expo
3. Computer Training Program
4. Educational Scholarships
5. Child Development Program
6. Housing Development
7. Business Initiatives

The first four objectives would be short range, and the last three objectives would be considered as long range plans. While the people who are members of the Canaan Church will be strengthened by this ministry, the primary emphasis is on helping the people that William Julius Wilson refers to as "the truly disadvantaged."

B. CHURCH FAMILY EXPO

In March 1992, Canaan's Community Development Corporation sponsored an event for minority entrepreneurs called Canaan's Family Expo. The primary purpose of the Expo was to give the entrepreneurs an opportunity to develop their businesses and network with other business owners in the Canaan family and community. Forty-two businesses were represented, which included service entities providing blood pressure screenings and information on public safety; there were caterers, photographers, and businesses selling cosmetics, jewelry, clothing, books and automobiles. Each business was assigned a booth to display products and services. People mingled and visited the various booths, some out of curiosity and others who had a genuine interest in doing business. An attempt was made to have a variety of booths at the Expo which would appeal to all ages in the community. A face painting booth and coloring contest was available for younger children.

The Expo was held from 10:00 a.m. to 6:00 p.m. on a Saturday. More than 2,000 people attended throughout the day. Announcements were made during morning service for approximately two months prior to the event, promoting the Expo. Members of the church were given the opportunity to submit an application to secure a booth four to six weeks prior to other businesses in the community. Public service announcements were made via radio and newspapers two weeks prior to and continuously up to the date of the Expo. An advertisement was also taken out in a local Christian and an African American newspaper.

A survey was completed by the participants after the Expo, which indicated the following results:

1) The average participant generated business both during and after the Expo, which resulted in sales ranging

from $75.00 (in desserts) to $27,000 (in auto/vehicle sales).

2) The majority of the businesses promoted at the Expo were not the primary sources of income for the participants.

3) Many of the businesses represented are located in Louisville's West end community.

4) The overwhelming response by the majority of the participants was that the Expo provided exposure and opportunities to develop business which many of the participants would not have had otherwise.

5) Participants were not charged a fee for a booth and most indicated they would not have been able to afford the cost normally associated with similar exhibits.

6) All of the entrepreneurs surveyed indicated that the benefits that the Expo provided far exceeded monetary rewards. Benefits ranged from increased exposure, experience and self confidence to opportunities for networking and comradery among fellow church members who are entrepreneurs.

C. COMPUTER LITERACY AND EDUCATION PROGRAM

As we move toward the twenty-first century, computer literacy will be required for persons to compete in the market economy. Canaan's Community Development Corporation initiated a computer training program to enhance the employability of people in our community. The goal of the program is to raise the computer literacy level of the community. Students receive instruction designed to upgrade their skills and employability.

The plan for education and training is comprised of two phases. These phases accommodate the different skills levels of the students.

Phase I - Computer Literacy Training is designed for beginners. It is a leveled approach which increases in complexity as one moves to the next course. Each course is an hour in length with the exception of keyboarding skills, which is available each week at a self-paced level. Courses may only be taken through the six-week cycle.

Phase I - Computer Literacy Training

> Introduction to Computers and Their Environments

> Learning Keyboarding Skills

> Keyboarding Practice
> Choosing Software Applications

> Introduction to DOS

> Introduction to Windows

Phase II - Employability Enhancement Training is designed for intermediate to advanced level users. The classes may be taken individually, however, a pre-test will be given to all persons who wish to take the Part 2 Course and exempt the Part 1 Course. Each application introduction class is one hour and is used as a prerequisite to each application level. Part 1 and 2 courses will be four hours individually.

Phase II - Employability Enhancement Training

Introduction to Word Processing
Part 1 - WordPerfect 5.1
Part 2 - WordPerfect 5.1

Part 1 - Microsoft Word 5.0
Part 2 - Microsoft Word 5.0

Introduction to Spreadsheets
Part 1 - Lotus 123v2.3
Part 2 - Lotus 123v2.3
Part 1 - Microsoft Excel 4.0
Part 2 - Microsoft Excel 4.0

Introduction to Desktop Publishing
Part 1 - Aldus PageMaker 4.0
Part 2 - Aldus PageMaker 4.0
Part 1 - First Publisher
Part 2 - First Publisher

Introduction to Presentation Media
Part 1 - Aldus Persuasion 2.0
Part 2 - Aldus Persuasion 2.0
Part 1 - Harvard Graphics 3.0
Part 2 - Harvard Graphics 3.0

Introduction to Database Management
Part 1 - Symantec Q&A
Part 2 - Symantec Q&A

Introduction to Integrated Software
Part 1 - Microsoft Works 2.0
Part 2 - Microsoft Works 2.0

The Computer Literacy and Education Program is administered according to the following staffing design, class schedules and enrollment guidelines:

Staffing Design - The staff will consist initially of a Director of Education and Training, two computer instructors, and one administrative assistant. (As the demand for training increases, instructors will also increase.)

The responsibilities of each staff person are as follows:

Director: Design, train and maintain the educational curriculum and goals for the program. Coordinate the training and instructors' schedules according to availability. Document program information for assessment and review by Canaan's Community Development Corporation.

Instructors: Demonstrate high level of software training and application knowledge. Train and maintain student records for classroom training. Follow curriculum outline for classroom training as designed by Director. Work closely with student body to ensure educational goals are being met. Provide support or substantive sessions as needed.

Administrator: Provide reception to the training program through enrollment and matriculation from the program. Complete necessary correspondence to students, certifying agents and other program related concerns. Issue certification to completing students and make phone calls to students to schedule and/or cancel sessions, as needed.

Once all staff persons were assigned, the educational process began to emerge.

Class Schedules: Classes will be offered in two phases. Phase I courses are designed to cover a six-week period of one-hour sessions. Phase II courses are designed to accommodate student preference in a nine-week period of four-hour sessions. Concurrent with all classroom training are practice sessions that will only be scheduled according to interest and availability. Class offerings are posted on a monthly basis in various media to encourage enrollment.

Enrollment Guidelines: Enrollment is as important to the success of the Computer Literacy and Education Program as is the quality of education. In order to accommodate periods of low enrollment, classes are offered only when class size has reached four or more students. Students can enroll for either the six-week or nine-week program. Only after they have completed each session will certification be issued, thereby holding students accountable for attendance. Since attendance is important to the success of the program, several incentives are awarded during the program to keep student's interest level high.

✝   ✝   ✝

The plight of Black America is still characterized by social and economic injustice. While there are some wealthy Black celebrities and other Black families that could be categorized as middle class, the masses of Black people are still living in economic deprivation.

Who is going to represent the oppressed? Who is going to speak and fight for those who have no voice in the market place? Civil rights organizations like the N.A.A.C.P. and Urban League have their role in the struggle, and must continue to challenge government and corporate America to act justly.

124

During the period of 1955-1968, the Black church played a leading role in the civil rights movement. An example of this was the Montgomery bus boycott that was effective for 381 days. The question before us today is, "Are we satisfied with sitting on the front of the bus, or do we want to own our own bus company?" The Black leadership of the civil rights movement grappled with difficult issues as they sought to break down walls of racism and discrimination so that Black people could fully participate in the mainstream of a market economy.

As we seek to build upon this foundation, we must continue to challenge the present social and economic system to be restructured into an egalitarian model so that America can become an inclusive community. I take this position because America has been developed on the back of Black labor. Black people have invested too much in this country for this generation or future generations not to demand its equal rights and position within the economy of this society. At the same time, we must continue to strongly advocate a sense of Black self-determination. We should place as much emphasis on economic empowerment as we do electoral politics. We should not allow our future to be determined by who sits in the White House or any other political seat. As a community, we must utilize the financial resources we have as good stewards and build our future by practicing collective economics, building our own institutions, and educating our children.

As we move toward the twenty-first century, the Black Liberation church will be a vital voice of Black America. The Black Liberation church is still the primary institution that carries the hopes and aspirations of the Black community. To speak of the church being involved in social, political, and economic issues may seem radical and out of place to some, but the Christ of the Gospels has a concern for the disinherited and dispossessed.

The Black church must continue to see the idea of liberation as being a major motif in the development of its ministries. In so doing, it incarnates the words of Christ spoken during the inauguration of His earthly ministry.

> The Spirit of the Lord is upon me, because he hath anointed me to preach the gospel to the poor; he hath sent me to heal the broken-hearted, to preach deliverance to the captives, and recovering of sight to the blind, to set at liberty them that are bruised, to preach the acceptable year of the Lord. Luke 4:18-19

Canaan's Community Development Corporation is an expression of this kind of liberating ministry.

WORKS CITED

1. Andrew Hacker, *Two Nations: Black and White, Separate, Hostile, Unequal* (New York: Charles Scribner's Sons, 1992), p. 102.

2. National Conference of Catholic Bishops, *Economic Justice For All: Pastoral Letter on Catholic Social Teaching and the U.S. Economy* (Washington: United States Catholic Conference, Inc., 1986), p. 8.

3. Paul L. Wachtel, *The Poverty of Affluence: A Psychological Portrait of the American Way of Life* (Philadelphia: New Society Publishers, 1989), p. 2.

4. David H. Swinton, *The Economic Status of African Americans: Permanent Poverty and Inequality*, ed. Janet Dewart (New York: National Urban League, 1991), p. 25.

5. *Ibid.*, p. 29.

6. Algonquin Parkway Community Needs Assessment Study Area (Louisville: 1989).

7. Swinton, op. cit., p. 30.

8. National Conference of Catholic Bishops, op. cit., p. 18.

9. Ronald J. Sider, *Rich Christians in an Age of Hunger* (Downers Grove, Illinois: Inter Varsity Press, 1984), p. 55.

10. Walter Brueggmann, Sharon Parks, Thomas H. Groome, *To Act Justly, Love Tenderly, Walk Humbly: An Agenda For Ministers* (Mahwah: Paulist Press, 1986), p. 8-9.

11. Thomas Hoyt, Jr., "The Biblical Tradition of the Poor and Martin Luther King, Jr.,"*The Journal of The I.T.C.*, Vol. IV (Spring, 1977), p. 18.

12. Jim Wallis, *Agenda for Biblical People* (New York: Harper and Row Publishers, 1976), p. 3.

13. National Conference of Catholic Bishops, op. cit., p. 28.

14. Aquinata Bockmann, "What Does the New Testament Say About the Church's Attitude to the Poor?" *The Poor And The Church*, eds. Norbert Greinacher and Alois Muller (New York: The Seabury Press, 1977), pp. 43-44.

15. Rhodes Thompson, *Stewards Shaped By Grace: The Church's Gift to a Troubled World* (St. Louis: Christian Board of Publication Press, 1990), p. 6.

16. M. Douglas Meeks, *God The Economist* (Minneapolis: Fortress Press, 1989), p. 33.

17. *Ibid.*, p. 56.

18. John Francis Kavanaugh, *Following Christ In A Consumer Society* (Maryknoll, New York: Orbis Books, 1981), p. 5.

19. Jawanza Kunjufu, *Black Economics: Solutions For Economic and Community Empowerment* (Chicago: African American Images, 1991), pp. 13-14.

20. Kavanaugh, op. cit., p. 98.

21. Max Weber, *The Protestant Ethic and the Spirit of Capitalism* (New York: Charles Scribner's Sons, 1958), p. 176-177.

22. *Ibid.*, p. 179.

23. James Cone, *Liberation: A Black Theology of Liberation* (Philadelphia: J. B. Lippincott Company, 1970), p. 41.

24. Howard Thurman, *Jesus and The Disinherited* (Indianapolis: Friends United Press, 1981), p. 23.

25. Theodore Walker, Jr., *Empower The People: Social Ethics for the African-American Church* (New York: Orbis Books, 1991), p. 35.

26. *Ibid.*, p. 35.

27. Kenneth L. Smith and Ira G. Zepp, Jr., *Search for the Beloved Community: The Thinking of Martin Luther King, Jr.* (Valley Forge: Judson Press, 1974), p. 123.

28. *Ibid.*, p. 126.

29. Joseph R. Washington, Jr., *Black Religion* (Boston: Beacon Press, 1964), p. 33.

30. Gayraud S. Wilmore, *Black Religion And Black Radicalism* (Maryknoll, New York: Orbis Books, 1983), p. 1.

31. *Ibid.*, p. 1.

32. C. Eric Lincoln and Lawrence H. Mamiya, *The Black Church in the African American Experience* (Durham, North Carolina: Duke University Press, 1990), p. 237.

33. Lerone Bennett, Jr., *Before The Mayflower: A History Of Black America* (Chicago: Johnson Publishing Company, Inc., 1982), pp. 222-223.

34. C. Eric Lincoln and Lawrence H. Mamiya, op. cit., p. 241.

35. W. E. Burghardt DuBois, *Economic Co-Operation of Negro Americans* (Atlanta: Atlanta University Press, 1907), p. 25.

36. Lerone Bennett, Jr., *The Shaping of Black America* (Chicago: Johnson Publishing Company, 1975), p. 313.

37. Otis Moss, "Black Church Distinctives," *The Black Christian Experience*, ed. Emmanuel L. McCall (Nashville: Broadman Press, 1972), p. 15.

38. Peter J. Paris, *The Social Teaching of the Black Churches* (Philadelphia: Fortress Press, 1985), pp. 69-70.

39. Leon H. Sullivan, *Build Brother Build* (Philadelphia: Macrae Smith Company, 1969), p. 78.

40. Otis Moss, "The Black Church Revolution," *The Black Christian Experience*, ed. Emmanuel L. McCall (Nashville: Broadman Press, 1972), p. 101.

41. Ralph Ellison, *Invisible Man* (New York: Vintage Books, 1981), p. 3.

42. William A. Jones, Jr., "Confronting the System," *African American Religious Studies*, ed. Gayraud S. Wilmore (Durham: Duke University Press, 1989), pp. 432-433.

43. Wayne G. Bragg, "From Development to Transformation," *The Church in Response to Human Need*, eds. Vinay Samuel and Chris Saugden (Grand Rapids: William B. Eerdmans Publishing Company, 1987), p. 38.

44. *Ibid.*, pp. 39-40.

45. Vishal Mangalwaldi, "Compassion and Social Reform: Jesus the Troublemaker," *The Church in Response to Human Need*, eds. Vinay Samuel and Chris Sugden (Grand Rapids: William B. Eerdmans Publishing Company, 1987), p. 193.

46. Cornel West, *Prophesy Deliverance: An Afro-American Revolutionary Christianity* (Philadelphia: The Westminister Press, 1982), p. 19.

47. William A. Jones, Jr., "Confronting the System," *African American Religious Studies*, ed. Gayraud S. Wilmore (Durham: Duke University Press, 1989), p. 439.

48. Theodore Walker, Jr., op. cit., p. 73.

49. Robert Michael Franklin, *Liberating Visions: Human Fulfillment and Social Justice in African-American Thought* (Minneapolis: Fortress Press, 1990), p. 75.

50. *Ibid.*, p. 79.

51. *Ibid.*, p. 87.

52. Peter J. Paris, *Black Religious Leaders: Conflict In Unity* (Louisville: Westminster and John Knox Press, 1991), p. 220.

53. *Ibid.*, p. 221-222.

54. Peter J. Paris, *Black Religious Leaders: Conflict in Unity* (Louisville: Westminster and John Knox Press, 1991), p. 71.

55. *Ibid.*, p. 83.

56. Joseph H. Jackson, *Unholy Shadows and Freedom's Holy Light* (Nashville: Townsend Press, 1967), p. 195.

57. Robert Michael Franklin, op. cit., p. 117.

58. Martin Luther King, Jr., *Strength To Love* (Philadelphia: Fortress Press, 1981), p. 103.

59. Robert Michael Franklin, op. cit., p. 129.

60. Paulo Freire, *Pedagogy of the Oppressed* (New York: Continuum Publishing Corporation, 1970), pp. 53-54.

61. Elliott D. Lee, "Churches Building Heaven On Earth: Rough times have spurred black churches to new economic and political activism," *Black Enterprise*, August, 1981, p. 35.

62. *Ibid.*, p. 35.

63. Angelo B. Henderson and Janice Hayes, "Who speaks for Black America?: Church, a force in rebuilding souls and cities," *Detroit News and Free Press*, August 9, 1992, p. 1, col 1.

64. *Ibid.*, p. 14, col 2.

65. David Osborne, "A Poverty Program That Works," *The New Republic*, May 8, 1989, p. 22.

66. V. P. Franklin, *Black Self-Determination: A Cultural History of the Faith of the Fathers* (Westport: Lawrence Hill & Company, 1984), p. 205.

67. Barbara Reynolds, "Blacks should use their billions to call their own shots," *U.S.A. Today*, July 31, 1992, p. 9A.